What People are saying about

How to Gain the Professional Edge

"Sue Morem is the leading expert on professionalism. Her new book is full of practical information that is a must read for anyone who wants to succeed in business." —**Frank A. Russell, President, Excellence in Training Corporation**

"At last, a book that contains vital and timely information concerning achieving your career goals. This book is a must read for everyone who wants to attain career success without having to go through the school of hard knocks. Sue Morem equips you with the tools and techniques necessary during this time of radical and drastic change to enhance your visibility and recognition in the organization to rapidly advance your career." —**Helena C. Douglas, Management Development Director, Clemson University**

"*How to Gain the Professional Edge* does an excellent job presenting information and insights critical to success in the workplace. The real world examples are right on target, and they powerfully substantiate the general principles underlying the text. I would recommend this book to individuals preparing to enter their careers—it succinctly describes what to do (and not to do) in professional interpersonal situations, but more importantly, perhaps, it thoughtfully explains why. The book will also be helpful to individuals seeking to revitalize and move ahead in their professional lives. This book will definitely be on the recommended reading list for our business students." —**Jerry Rinehart, Director of Undergraduate Studies, Carlson School of Management, University of Minnesota**

"Sue's material was well received and the evaluations from her students were excellent. Sue's presentation makes learning a positive and enjoyable experience." —**Susan Mortenson, Training Coordinator, Honeywell**

"Susan's keen insights and personal experience are evident all through the book. She identifies all of the 'points of difference' essential for winning presentations." —**Richard L. Knowlton, Chairman, The Hormel Foundation**

"Ms. Morem's views are timely and invaluable in today's rapidly changing business climate. She shares with her readers a common sense approach to workplace behavior. This is a must read for anyone serious about success." —**Mark A. Cohn, Chairman and Chief Executive Officer, Damark International, Inc.**

"Nothing is more powerful in service than the instantaneous impression customers get the first time they come in contact with your organization. The most powerful impact comes from your employees who are, in the customers' minds, the organization. In her book, *How to Gain the Professional Edge*, Sue Morem has captured the essence of that first impression and shares the tools to make that ever-important moment not only dazzling but unforgettable." —**Petra A. Marquart, Author, *The Power of Service***

"A crucial area of concern for today's executive, thoroughly presented by the most recognized expert in the field." —**Randall Goodden, Vice President, Everbrite Inc., author and international speaker**

"Extremely helpful and informative. The information is of great interest and she shares wonderful material." —**Jon S. Carlson, Vice President of Income Development, American Cancer Society**

"Sue's new book provides insightful advice that we all can implement in our business and daily lives. *How to Gain the Professional Edge* will be required reading for our whole team." —**Mark R. Mudra, President and CEO, Home Water**

"Sue and her powerful message are a driving force behind many successful careers. Must reading for anyone looking for a formula that magnitudes their dreams." —**Kay Lewis, Executive Producer, La Jolla Project Production Company**

"Susan's presentation was superb! She demonstrates a great deal of professionalism, mixed with a wonderful sense of humor. Her material is up-to-date and appropriate for any audience." —**Maurice Chenier, Operations Manager, Ceridian Corporation**

"I have been active in the Minnesota business community for over 40 years. During that time I have met many successful business men and women, from all levels of management, including CEO's from several of Minnesota's top 100 companies. I have not met one who didn't follow the basics which Sue's book outlines plainly, and understandably. *How to Gain the Professional Edge* is a must read for success. Thanks for writing it, Sue!" —**Henry Kristal, Co-owner, Embers Restaurants**

"Our associates responded well to Sue's message which was both informational and entertaining. She has helped us to develop insight and awareness, which was our goal." —**Donald R. Melton, Senior Vice President, Resident Manager, Dain Bosworth, Incorporated**

"As a result of using the information in Sue's book, our employees are treating each other more respectfully and professionally. Consequently, we are having more fun and our service has improved dramatically. Sue's book offers answers to problems and provides a successful plan to use for anyone looking to succeed." —**Randy Stanley, General Manager, Ruth's Chris Steak House**

"The enthusiastic manner in which Sue presents her information makes learning fun. It is evident that she believes in the importance of being at your personal best at all times." —**Jean Johnson, 3M, Office Supervisor**

"The reason I like Sue Morem's work is that she's a good teacher of something in short supply today: people skills." —**Letitia Baldrige, Author of the *New Complete Guide to Executive Manners***

"Sue Morem walks her talk. She looks more pulled together for a casual lunch than most people look at the Oscars! Her warm, witty presentations instruct and inspire and this great book does too!" — **Susan Vass, Author, Speaker, Comedian**

"Image and presence are an integral part of every professional success story. Unfortunately very little of value is available. With *How to Gain the Professional Edge*, Susan Morem rights this wrong and will help you climb higher on the ladder of success." —**Martin Yate, Author of the *Knock 'em Dead* job hunting books**

HOW TO

GAIN

THE

Professional

EDGE

Achieve the Personal and Professional Image You Want

BY SUSAN MOREM

Better Books

How to Gain the Professional Edge—Achieve the Personal and Professional Image You Want

Morem, Susan E.
   How to Gain the Professional Edge—Achieve the Personal and Professional Image You Want/Susan Morem

   p. cm.

ISBN 1-886656-04-5

Library of Congress Catalog
Card Number: 96-79567

1. Business   2. Image
3. Self Help   4. Careers
5. Marketing   I. Title

Printed and bound in the United States of America.

99 98 97 96   10 9 8 7 6 5 4 3 2 1

HOW TO
GAIN
THE
Professional
EDGE

Table of Contents

Acknowledgments

I am grateful for the support and encouragement given to me by so many people. This book would not have become a reality without them.

Thank you to: Jody Majeres, for design services, Kristine Anderson, for page layout, Laurie Turnquist for editing services and Kathie Anderson for proof reading.

A special thanks to my personal "coaches", Kathie Bortnem, Kay Newberg, and Jill Spiegel; for your friendship, honesty, feedback and support given to me over the years.

My thanks goes to friends, colleagues, clients and to the hundreds of business people who have attended my workshops and seminars over the years. You have given me motivation in my work and have been an inspiration in writing this book.

To the very special people in my life, I offer my thanks:

To my mother- and father-in-law, Bev and Chuck Morem, for always asking for copies of my work to "show off" to everyone. Your pride in me and my accomplishments mean more than you know.

To my sister, Eileen Levin, for your open ear and the sometimes painfully honest feedback that only a sister can give.

To my parents, Rose and Jules Levin, who always believed I could accomplish anything I wanted. You are the best teachers and role models. I'll never stop learning from you and the standards you have set.

To my incredible three daughters, Stephanie, Stacie and Samantha, for reminding me that success shows up in many ways—you are my greatest success in life and my pride and joy.

And finally, to my husband Steve, who saw all of my potential and believed in me even before I saw it in myself. You have always been there to encourage and support me in everything I do and are my biggest fan. This book is dedicated to you.

Introduction

Total Quality Management. Downsize. Streamline. Restructure. We're all running as fast as we can to keep up with the changes in business and within our own fields of expertise. But it seems that something critical is getting lost in the shuffle, specifically how we should act—toward our bosses, peers, employees, customers, and colleagues—as we embrace the "new" workplace.

In our quest to keep up with the times and to gain the professional edge, many of us are uncertain about the most important factor in the success we're after—the way we should handle ourselves with other people.

Studies have shown that *93 percent of what is believed about people in business is based upon visual messages,* not on credentials or on the content of conversation. This means that the way you handle yourself and others, your people skills, enthusiasm, and the leadership qualities you possess—and display—are even more critical to your career success than your technical or professional expertise.

Assuming that you have the skills and expertise to do your job, how do you develop the ability to work and interact with others in a way that sets you apart from the rest?

How To Gain the Professional Edge was written to help answer a host of questions about behavior, attitude, and presence. The answers to these questions will help you become a person with that special something that people remember and gain the skills that open doors along the way. By reading the book and working through the exercises provided, you will learn what you need to know to improve your professionalism. But you'll only gain as much from this book as you are willing to put into it. Take the time to read, think, and really work through the suggested exercises to get the most from this book.

People often ask me how I got into the business of helping others. My career began when I took out my first business loan at age 18 to sell Mary Kay cosmetics, and 2 years later I left college to sell Dale Carnegie courses. I chose to do this because I truly believed in the concepts these courses taught. I had taken the course myself and highlighted more in Carnegie's book, *How To Win Friends and Influence People* than I ever did in any classroom textbook. It was not easy to convince people to take a course in self-improvement and I spent most of my time cold-calling without making many sales. I knew, however, that the experience I gained would be invaluable and I was determined to stick with it for at least a year, which I did. After that I became a manufacturer's representative and was fortunate enough to achieve success. I won a number of awards, and regularly exceeded my quotas and sales goals.

It wasn't that I was smarter or worked harder than my peers. In fact, with three young children at home, I was in the difficult position of balancing home and career. Yet, I was able to excel. I realized the one thing I could do best was "sell" myself; my customers and colleagues enjoyed doing business with me.

I decided to parlay my skills into a business—Premier Presentation Inc.—to show others how they, too, are responsible for their own success. Everywhere, I've found that people want to know how to get along better, and be more productive, with other people. When I started my business, I knew achieving success would be difficult. I prepared myself to expect that for every 20 calls I made, perhaps one person might be interested in hiring me. I had to gather all of my courage to get on the phone to contact companies. However, I found that once I learned to ask the right questions and meet people face-to-face, a pattern emerged. I heard the same comments over and over again:

> "I've got this talented person…smart, hard working…would love to promote her, but I can't. She doesn't look the part of management," or "He doesn't present himself well," "She can't communicate effectively."

I've even had managers tell me, "He looks outdated; she shuffles her feet; he slurps his coffee."

In fact, it is often so difficult for managers to confront these issues that I have made presentations to a group of 30 because one person needed to hear the message.

In order to make the workshops a success and to help the companies that hire me reach their objectives, I spend a significant amount of time helping the company decide how to introduce the concept of a professionalism workshop to their employees in order to avoid the frequent apprehension many of the attendees have about participating. Therefore, I want to make sure I spend some time with you, upfront, to help you understand the objectives of this book, and how you can benefit from it whether you are a seasoned professional or a newcomer to the business world.

Invariably, there are at least three categories most people fall into. There are the people who are excited about any opportunity to learn something new and are eager to pick up a few new ideas and learn more about themselves. These people attend workshops with a good attitude, an open mind, and participate eagerly. They usually pick up a few new ideas and are able to implement them into their lives.

There are also people who attend, but aren't sure if it's a worthy investment of their time because they believe they are already successful, know about professionalism, and would rather be doing something else they consider more productive. The people in this category usually say that they picked up a few good pointers but most of it was a good reminder and refresher course in basic common sense.

And then there are people who attend only because they have to. They don't want to be there and can't understand why their company would waste its money and time having the workshop in the first place. These people are sure they won't learn anything new or gain anything from the session, and because they generally refuse to participate and expend most of their energy resisting anything that takes place, they fulfill their prophecy.

Perhaps you fall into one of these three categories. Maybe someone gave you this book and you wonder why. It could be required reading by your manager or teacher. Or maybe you are interested in picking up any new ideas you can and are reading this because you chose to. No matter what the reason, you can benefit from this book.

When I ask people to explain what professionalism is, most people define a "professional" as someone who has an important position with an impressive title, who earns a high salary, wears power suits and occupies a large office. I have found that there are many people who exemplify professionalism who are far from the image described.

When I think of people I have met over the years, there is one person who has impressed me, who I often speak about, and he didn't have a big title, earn a lot of money or wear expensive clothing. This person made a lasting impression on me because he exceeded my expectations and exemplified my interpretation of a true "professional".

He held what some of you may consider to be a menial position, but he acted as though it was the most important one there was. I first encountered him on my way to work when I went to the drive-through of a local Burger King. If you've ever ordered food drive-through style, I am sure you will agree that it is usually not an overwhelming experience. It hadn't been for me until that day. An energetic, pleasant voice boomed over the intercom as he said "Good morning, welcome to Burger King. How may I help you?" I was a bit taken with this unusually perky greeting and immediately drew the conclusion that the manager must be filling in for an employee. I ordered my coffee, went to the window to pay, and got a good look at the young man who continued to smile, move quickly, and look me in the eyes as he sincerely thanked me for my business and wished me a good day. It turned out that he was not the manager, but an employee who took his job seriously, and for the next few months I looked forward to my drive-through trips and continued to receive the same fabulous treatment. He remembered my name, the fact that I took cream with my coffee, and even recognized my voice. One day, back at my office, I noticed an 800 number on the bag my food came in that solicited feedback on how they were doing. I was so moved by the level of service and the attitude of this person that I took the time to call the number to tell the main office about this wonderful person who worked for them. Now I, much like you, am a busy person and rarely take the time to call with a complaint, let alone a compliment, but I was so impressed by his service and character that I wanted to do something to show my appreciation so that he might benefit from it. I made the call simply to say how great he was.

Eventually, he left, and wasn't there to greet me anymore. I can only assume that he was promoted or moved on to fulfill whatever career goals he desired. But he made a lasting impression on me and everywhere I go I tell this story about him because very few people have exceeded my expectations the way he did. Maybe it was because he went so far *beyond* my expectations that I was so impressed. He had a profound effect on me. Think about the effect you have on the people you come into contact with everyday. What impact do you have on them? When you are gone from your place of work, what will people remember about you?

Chances are, whether you are a seasoned professional or a newcomer, in addition to some new tips you will pick up, it is also likely there will be information in this book that will reinforce things you already know. Developing your professionalism is an on-going process and is something that comes naturally to very few people. The people you know who are polished and professional work at it, just as they work at improving any other aspect of their job. No matter where you are in your career, it is important to step back and evaluate yourself every now and then. After reading this book, your awareness of yourself and the way people act will increase. This is the beginning of the on-going process.

Personal image and habits are a sensitive issue. We often miss cues others are giving us because we don't want to hear what they have to say. But missing these cues could destroy your career. Don't miss opportunities or be the one who is bypassed because of the way you eat, dress, or behave. These are all things that are within your control.

The business world is changing everyday. Advances in technology, the wide acceptance and popularity of dressing casually for work, and the new ways of interacting with others all signify a break with the traditional ways of doing business in the past. It is essential that you are aware of these changes as they occur and do what's necessary to stay ahead of the competition.

Yet there are some things that are timeless. Treating others well, looking and acting your best, and a positive attitude will never lose their importance. These aspects of professionalism are critical to your success.

As you read this book, you can learn to take control of the way you present yourself and to give yourself every advantage to succeed. You can begin to have a greater appreciation about what works in business and what those extra qualities are that will show you how to gain the professional edge.

Critical First Impressions

Throughout this book, you will have the opportunity to analyze, understand, and refine your professional image. Many people believe that the image they project simply *is* and exists independently of who they really are. They assume their image is out of their direct control. This book will prove that *nothing could be further from the truth.*

Your professional image is made up of five key components:

Impression
Movement
Attitude
Grooming
Etiquette

Whether consciously or unconsciously, each of us is sending a message about who we are every time we interact with another human being. This book is about learning how to consciously manage your message for maximum impact and personal success.

Did you know?

- 93 percent of what is believed about you in business is based upon visual, not verbal messages.

- Your effectiveness and confidence increase when you are consistently well-dressed.

- The image you project is directly attributed to your product or service.

- Productivity can be increased up to 20 percent by presenting an effective professional image.

- Your visual appearance and your professional manner are among your most powerful and accessible business skills. Use them to your advantage!

Before we go any further, take a moment to reflect on your knowledge and beliefs about what it takes to excel in today's business environment. The following exercises will give you an opportunity to explore your own attitudes and beliefs and help you begin to assess your professionalism. Please read the following statements and circle whether you agree or disagree with each one. Don't worry if you're uncertain about some of these statements. They are addressed at the end of the chapter with a thorough discussion of each.

1. How you come across is more important than what you say or do.   True/False

2. The longer you are at a job, the less important your appearance becomes.   True/False

3. If you want to be noticed or to be sure that your on-the-job contributions are recognized, dress to stand out.   True/False

4. Less than 10 percent of verbal communication is actually made through the spoken word. True/False

5. We draw long lasting conclusions about people within the first few seconds of meeting them.
                                                   True/False

6. You can tell a lot about someone by the condition of his or her shoes.   True/False

7. You never have a second chance to make a first impression.   True/False

8. It takes a lot of money to look and be successful.
                                                   True/False

9. There is one—and only one—basic look of success, and all successful people adhere to it.   True/False

10. There are two distinct standards of behavior—one for men and one for women.   True/False

Evaluating Who You Are and Where You Want to Go

This book is designed to be your own workbook. One of the most important things to do is to stop and think about what has brought you to where you are today. In order to get started, you need to evaluate who you are and where you want to go.

Before you can manage your message, you need to understand what message you're sending. Do you know how others see you? Do you know how you *want* them to see you? Is your personal image consistent with the "norms" for appearance and behavior in your profession? What is your definition of "success?" Do you consider *yourself* a success?

Personal Evaluation

1. Describe yourself (in three words) as you see yourself.

   1. _____
   2. _____
   3. _____

2. Describe yourself (in three words) as you would like to see yourself.

   1. _____
   2. _____
   3. _____

3. What changes (if any) do you need to make in your life, your image, or your actions so that the above two sets of descriptions match—in other words, so that you *are* what you want to be?

   _____
   _____
   _____
   _____
   _____

4. What are your three greatest strengths? *Capitalize these to remind yourself to capitalize on them. Know what you're good at.*

   1. _____
   2. _____
   3. _____

5. What are three areas you could improve?
    1. _____
    2. _____
    3. _____

6. What makes you great at your job or at what you do?

    _____

    _____

    _____

    _____

7. Do you often apologize for your appearance? Yes/No

8. When you pass a mirror, do you try to avoid looking because you don't like what you see?   Yes/No

9. Is dressing each day a negative experience?   Yes/No

10. Does it take you more than 30 minutes to get ready each day?   Yes/No

11. Do you feel people underestimate your ability?
                                                Yes/No

12. Are you dissatisfied with your current weight?
                                                Yes/No

13. Do you feel uncomfortable in social situations, unsure about how to introduce yourself and uneasy making conversation?   Yes/No

14. Do you feel awkward in new situations?   Yes/No

15. Do you become uptight under pressure?   Yes/No

16. Do you feel rushed and stressed much of the time?
                                                Yes/No

17. Do you find that people frequently misunderstand you?   Yes/No

18. Do you often regret what you've said or obsessively rethink how you could have handled a person or situation more effectively?   Yes/No

As you look back on your answers, you'll begin to see that your image of yourself and how you present yourself is an integral part of your sense of self-confidence and self-esteem. Do you find it easier to list your strengths, or your weaknesses? Do you find agreement between the way you see yourself and the way you would like others to see you, or not?

The key to presenting a professional image is something you've probably heard before: "accentuate the positive." To be successful and to project a successful image you *must* know what your strengths are, and be proud to name and develop them. If you have trouble coming up with answers to these questions, *work* on them—know what makes you great! If *you* don't know, no one else will.

Write each of the strengths you've listed in bold letters on a 3" x 5" card and tape it to your mirror, or the sun visor of your car, or in the front of a book you look at daily. Do whatever it takes to remind yourself of *what's good about you* and what *you*—and *only you*—have to offer.

Before you can gain the professional edge, you need to believe you are successful. Once you feel successful, the tips and tactics in this book are simply icing on the cake—the ways to ensure that your outside image matches the confident, successful image you have inside.

You Never Have a Second Chance to Make a First Impression

Many theories explain that the way you present yourself affects perceived job performance and career success. In a job interview, for instance, the interviewer often decides *within moments* whether or not you are a serious candidate for the job. You don't have much time to establish your credibility or your expertise. A stellar résumé, years of experience, even the right contacts, may not overcome the weak handshake, the inappropriate attire, the ungrammatical or awkward comment made in these critical moments of initial judgment.

If credentials were all that mattered, why would an interview take place at all? Many qualified people have equal skills and ability, but in an interview, each person can be assessed for how he or she looks, acts, speaks, reacts, and ultimately, how he or she will fit the image of the company.

You don't have to let simple mistakes in clothing or personal presentation obscure your natural gifts and talents. You don't have to give a potential employer a superficial reason not to hire or promote you.

The following story illustrates the impact first impressions can have and how those impressions can, to some degree, be controlled by a confident professional attitude in the face of apparent obstacles and problems.

Early in my career as a speaker, I had an opportunity to address a group of employees on the topic of "Professionalism and the Critical First Impression."

On the morning of this particular talk, I felt especially confident and well prepared, and left in plenty of time (I thought) to arrive at the conference center 30 minutes ahead of the 8 a.m. meeting time.

I followed the directions I'd received to the letter but I became concerned when, after a left turn, nothing looked familiar. I pulled over and called my client who told me that the directions I had been given were wrong.

It was time to backtrack—in rush-hour traffic! I finally pulled into the parking lot at ten minutes *after* eight. A large picture window in the conference room faced the parking lot, and through it I peered at 25 of the most humorless-looking people I'd ever seen, each of them watching my every move.

I suddenly had a feat to accomplish for which, in all my diligent planning, I had *not* prepared: overcoming the very negative first impression this room full of people had of me.

"Good morning," I said with a smile and as much enthusiasm as I could muster. "I'm here today to talk about professionalism and first impressions!" Silence.

"What impression do you all have of *me* right now?" I went on bravely. A few faces started to loosen up, not in *smiles*, exactly, but not scowls either.

"Have you ever had something go wrong, in spite of careful planning and preparation?" Some heads started to nod.

"Have you ever made a mistake or had a problem get in your way?" Most of the faces were with me by now.

"I made a wrong turn on my way here this morning," I continued. "And that one wrong turn turned my whole morning upside down. I could let it destroy me, I could complain, I could let it get me down. But, wait a minute, isn't that exactly what we're here to talk about—how to work with problems while remaining professional?"

I related to them and encouraged them to relate to me and, most importantly, I communicated the message that professionalism isn't being something you're not, *it's being the best of who you are.* By being honest and open with them and admitting that I had made a mistake, I actually helped create a bond between us. I wasn't preaching to the group, but I was sharing a part of myself with them. It reinforced the fact that people like to deal with other people, not with robots. I took responsibility for what happened and didn't blame anyone but myself. People can be very forgiving and accepting when you admit a mistake. Finally, the experience reminded me how important it is to leave plenty of time to spare so that I will always be early and not have to go through an experience like that again.

We all have things that get in our way, that surprise us, or alter our expectations. How we *deal* with the problems and the surprises is the test. I *did* overcome that negative first impression, but it took some quick thinking, a lot of work, and a little luck. And you can be sure that group of people will *never* forget that I was late, and that their first impression of me, in spite of my very best intentions, was *not* a good one.

Factors of a First Impression

Think about meeting someone for the first time, perhaps in a job interview or making a presentation to a potential customer or client. What kind of impression would you like to make? What can you do (or not do) to convey that impression?

We make first impressions through both verbal and nonverbal communication. That part is fairly obvious. But you might be surprised by how many factors combine to convey an impression that is registered in just a few seconds or minutes at the most:

Verbal	Nonverbal
Tone of voice	Overall appearance
Choice of words	Posture
Attitude	Facial expressions
Rate of speech	Gestures
Enunciation	Clothing
	Hair

Many people believe that the impression they make is out of their control. Not true! Each of the factors listed above can be analyzed, practiced and ultimately—if you want it to be—changed. Developing and projecting the type of image you desire is a learned skill at which you must work like any other skill.

After the First Impression: Four Simple Rules that Guarantee Business Success

We live in an era of "anything goes," but don't be fooled. In business, there *are* rules, no less real for being unwritten or unspoken. And you can learn them:

Look the part.

Don't think you're giving up your individuality or compromising who you really are. Instead, you're being sensitive, savvy, and smart. To be successful, you have to project an image with which your clients, your employer and your colleagues are comfortable and it's simple human nature, however predictable it might seem, to feel most comfortable with people who look, more or less, *like us.*

The next time you enter a store or a party, pay attention to the clerk, or the dinner companion, you seek out. It is likely that you will gravitate toward those persons who look as if they can help you (in a store) or will be interesting to talk to (at a party). What makes them look approachable? Are they people of about your own age, educational level, and social and cultural background—in short, people who look like you?

We also tend to favor the *expected* over the unexpected in others' appearance. Would you be more likely to trust a doctor in a lab coat and stethoscope, or one (perhaps equally competent) dressed in shorts and sunglasses? Would you be more apt to hire a carpenter in coveralls and a tool belt or one wearing a sport coat and tie?

You actually have *more* latitude to "be yourself" and to contribute your particular skills and ideas when you look the part you want to play. By looking the part, you eliminate superficial barriers so other people can listen to what you have to say and accept what you have to contribute. When it comes to clothing and grooming, there are a few general, well-established, accepted guidelines that can help *anyone* enhance his or her look with attention to detail and up-to-date grooming and wardrobe tips.

Act the part.

If you think that etiquette has gone the way of white gloves and top hats, I've got news for you. Etiquette is really just a system of behaviors helping people know what to expect in situations where the company, or the locale, might be unfamiliar.

Most business people will, at some point, find themselves in the position of introducing colleagues to one another, hosting or attending a business function, or socializing with clients and colleagues on any number of occasions, to name just a few of the most common situations in which business etiquette has a role to play.

Knowing how to make other people feel comfortable, and feel comfortable about oneself in the process, is an art, and can make all the difference between being perceived as successful or unsuccessful. Etiquette is an art worth mastering if you are really serious about being successful in any field.

Understanding the role nonverbal communication, or "body language," plays in the way you come across is also a critical component of the art of etiquette.

Both etiquette and body language are discussed at length later in this book. You'll want to be in charge of both to gain the professional edge.

Be the part.

Although a particular suit, hairstyle or handshake can contribute to (or detract from) a personal style, your ability to demonstrate that you are capable, congenial, and constant will cinch the impression. Apply the "3 Cs Test" as a quick way to monitor and modulate your style as you encounter the various "audiences" and "theaters" of your working life:

Capable—Do you look and act like somebody who can do the job—not only the job you have, but the one you're striving toward?

Congenial—Do you look and act like someone your clients, customers, boss, and co-workers can talk to and work with? Are you sincere, approachable, friendly and helpful?

Consistent—Do you look and act trustworthy? Are you dependable, the kind of person others can count on?

The creative director of an ad agency, the attorney, and the manager of a high fashion retail store all need to come across as capable, congenial, and consistent *in their particular setting.* They are unlikely to dress or behave alike. But the ones who are successful *will* look, act and be *within the norm* for their particular industry and workplace.

You'll be more successful if you are attentive to what that norm is in the job you have or the job you want, and operate within it. It's that simple.

Think the part.

How you think about things such as change and risk also plays a key role in how successful you are in your work.

Change is something many resist, but change is a part of all aspects of our lives, at work and at home. We change our tastes, our friends, our interests, our jobs. Even in a downsizing situation, change can turn out to be the best thing for employees who must find a new job. Many people find new opportunities by changing careers, going into business for themselves, or just plain re-evaluating and fine-tuning their goals. Embrace change. Take it as a chance to change the way you're doing things, to grow and improve.

Risk is often the opportunity to experience great success by going beyond the ordinary. For example, I had long dreamed of becoming a business advice columnist. My public relations person gave me the number of the business editor of our local newspaper. I had to work with this editor for a full year writing sample columns, other articles, and calling him regularly. Finally, when another prominent columnist stopped writing a column, my window of opportunity opened. One phone call, and taking a big risk, forced me to stretch, step out of what I ordinarily did. The results were well worth it. Take risks. Don't let things happen to you, make them happen!

Points to Remember

1. You can control the image you project, and "manage your message" through Impression, Movement, Attitude, Grooming, and Etiquette.

2. You never have a second chance to make a first impression. Make the most of the only chance you get.

3. There are eleven verbal and nonverbal factors that affect the first impression that you make *and* the overall image you project. Learn to be aware of how you are communicating both verbally and nonverbally in each area.

4. *Look* the part. Your appearance should "fit in" with norms of your industry and workplace. Be known for your ideas and hard work, not your funny clothes or unusual hairstyle.

5. *Act* the part. Learn how to use a few simple rules of etiquette to put others at ease, and yourself on the track to success. Add to this a few principles of nonverbal communication to consciously control the way you "come across" to gain the professional edge.

6. *Be* the part. Master the 3 Cs: Capable, Congenial and Consistent.

7. *Think* the part. Take risks and welcome change so you can experience new ideas and adventures.

Questions and Answers:
What Does Your Image Say About You?

Here are the answers to the questions you asked yourself at the beginning of this chapter.

1. How you come across is more important than what you say or do.

   TRUE.
   A study conducted by Dr. Albert Mehrabian at UCLA showed that 93 percent of what is believed about people is based upon visual messages, not on credentials and not on the content of conversation. This means that the way you handle yourself and others, and the people skills, enthusiasm, and leadership qualities you possess and display are every bit as critical to your career success (if not more so) than technical or professional expertise.

2. The longer you are at a job, the less important your appearance becomes.

   FALSE.
   Your appearance is always important. You might think about it more when you "dress to impress" for a job interview or other important meeting, but once you have the job you should continue to take pride in your appearance. Most people simply feel better

when they look good. Have you ever noticed that on a day when you're feeling below par, you can elevate your mood by dressing yourself to look better than you feel? Try it sometime!

3. If you want to be noticed or to be sure that your on-the-job contributions are recognized, dress to stand out.

    FALSE.
    The goal is to dress to "fit in," not stand out. If your clothing is outrageous or controversial or simply inappropriate to the setting or situation, you are not noticed, your clothing is. You want your other qualities to stand out, and your clothing to support that.

4. Less than 10 percent of verbal communication is actually made through the spoken word.

    TRUE.
    Dr. Albert Mehrabian's study shows that only 7 percent of verbal communication is made through the spoken word. Therefore, focus less on what you say and more on how you say it. Children understand this when they play Simon Says. In that game, attention is paid to what Simon does rather than what he says, which is easy to do because we believe more of what we see than what we hear.

5. Long lasting conclusions are drawn about people within the first few seconds of meeting them.

    TRUE.
    Of course, you want to be valued for who you are, your deeper selves, yet you might never get the

chance if you fail to connect upfront. How you look, act, and come across is extremely important. Think for a moment about products you buy at the grocery store. Why do many people prefer brand names over generic? Something convinces you that food packaged attractively and familiarly tastes better. We've all had the experience of meeting someone with whom we clicked instantly—and someone else whom we disliked virtually on sight. First impressions! We all make them, and we all have them made about us.

6. You can tell a lot about someone by the condition of his or her shoes.

    TRUE.
    Human resources professionals say that they have learned to look at applicants' shoes for clues about their personalities. You can dress the part, but if it's not "head to toe," you reveal a lack of attention to detail and follow-through. Little things often do count. People, especially prospective employers, do pay attention to shoes. In face-to-face encounters, our eyes meet the eyes of the other person, then sweep down to the feet and back up to the face again. This happens so quickly, you may not be aware of it, but you do this with everyone you meet. So beware of the run in the nylon or dirty, unpolished, down-at-the-heel shoes; they will be noticed.

7. You never have a second chance to make a first impression.

    TRUE.
    First impressions are lasting impressions. Though it is possible to overcome a negative first impression

sooner or later, it takes as many as seven encounters with someone to change a bad first impression. That is why it's important for you to present the image you desire to help you achieve your objectives. You can make a favorable first impression and have a positive effect on those around you. If you take control of your image and manage the message that image conveys.

8. It takes a lot of money to look and be successful.

FALSE.
It is often assumed that it's costly to look successful, but money alone is not the determining factor. Learning to work with what you have and presenting yourself as a successful person is the key. While your clothing should be the best you can afford, your professional demeanor is just as important. Successful behaviors can be learned by anyone, regardless of income.

9. There is one—and only one—basic look of success, and all successful people adhere to it.

FALSE.
The cloned look in dress and personal appearance is a thing of the past. Today, you have more freedom in your choices and can generally dress in a way that expresses who you are within the bounds of what is appropriate for your particular occupation. When you feel comfortable with the way you look, you can extend that comfort to others. But there are still certain guidelines that provide a framework for creating your personal and professional image.

10. There are two distinct standards of behavior—one for men and one for women.

FALSE.

Though gender plays a part in all personal interactions, successful encounters are more likely to take place when gender is not an issue. For instance, instead of worrying about whether to open doors, shake hands, rise or remain seated, or tell an "off color" story, you should focus on courteous, professional and appropriate behavior. Under any circumstance, then, the gender of the person you are dealing with becomes completely unimportant.

CHAPTER

Do You Hear What You Are *Not* Saying?

Think of yourself as a gift that needs packaging. You're smart, skilled, competent, creative and highly motivated. You're willing to do a great job, and you have the talent to do it. That's the gift. But you're the only one who knows these things about you; telling others how wonderful you are in so many words just isn't going to be the right approach. You can think it, but can't say it!

So what is a good approach? Packaging yourself in a way that conveys a powerful presence is the right approach. Presence is basic to having the *professional edge*. You want others to know you're in charge. You want them to perceive you as more than just competent: you're able to handle any situation, be gracious, stay in control, be aware of subtleties and show your ability as a cool negotiator.

Read the statement and circle true or false. Then read through this chapter and compare your answers to the explanations at the end.

1. An effective handshake should involve at least four to five pumps up and down.   True/False

2. Smiling can make you appear friendly or influential.   True/False

3. Never look someone directly in the eyes—you risk being threatening or invading personal space.   True/False

4. Men should shake hands more gently with women than with other men.   True/False

5. Showing no expression can make you appear hostile or uninterested.   True/False

6. You will be perceived as more friendly and approachable when your body language is open (uncrossed arms and legs, directly facing the person you are talking with, pleasant facial expression, etc.).   True/False

7. Nervous gestures (hair twisting, finger tapping, etc.) are distracting to your message.   True/False

8. Sitting or standing up straight and holding your head high can increase your energy level. True/False

9. Body language often tells the truth, despite verbal communication.   True/False

Before you begin to work on using nonverbal communication to improve your image, consider for a moment the image you *don't* want to convey. Can you think of someone you have never felt comfortable with, someone you can't trust? Perhaps it's the way that person puts down others or monopolizes the conversation or often has a hidden agenda that replaces openness and honesty.

Now think of someone you admire. What qualities does this person possess? Try to picture them in your mind. Surely you want others to think of you as diplomatic, forceful and successful at solving problems. Now let's explore the elements of presence: how you stand, move and speak, and the verbal and nonverbal cues you give to others.

How To Stand, Move And Speak With Authority And Grace

As mentioned earlier, 93 percent of what is believed about us is visual. How much of your message do you think you convey through your body language, tone of voice and words? Many of us would answer this question by saying that most of our message is communicated through our words. Right? Wrong! When you break down communication, the division looks like this.

Body language sends *55 percent* of your message.
Tone of voice sends *38 percent* of your message.
Words send *7 percent* of your message.

Your message is conveyed through verbal, vocal and visual clues:

Visual...Your eye contact, facial expression, body
posture and gestures
Vocal...Your tone, pitch and rate of speech
Verbal...Your choice of words

Visual

Understanding Body Language

Through body language, we communicate our true feelings and reactions to people, places and things. Look at the list of responses below and decide which you convey and which you might need to work on:

Positive Responses...	**Negative Responses...**
Strong handshake	Limp, "dead fish" handshake
Leaning forward	Pulling back or turning away
Consistent eye contact	Shifting, darting eye movement
Smiling	Frowning, squinting
Relaxed, controlled body movements	Nervous, jerky body movements
Confident, upright posture	Slouched, hunched posture
Expressive face	Lack of expression
Uncrossed arms, legs	Arms and legs crossed
Tilted head	Rigid posture, no expression
Open hands, palms	Hands clenched together
Nodding up and down	Shaking head back and forth
Head held high	Looking down
Direct eye or face contact	Avoiding eye contact

Read the following and rate yourself: Always Sometimes Never

- My handshake is firm and brief.   1   2   3

- I sit upright with feet on the floor.   1   2   3

- I make eye contact at least 90   1   2   3
  percent of the time

- I smile often and with sincerity.   1   2   3

- I hold myself in an open and   1   2   3
  approachable way.

- I carry myself with confidence.   1   2   3

- I am aware of the expression on   1   2   3
  my face at all times.

Now that you've analyzed some of your body language, which areas do you think are your strengths and help you convey your message positively? Consider asking others for feedback. Most of us either avoid asking for feedback from others or just don't think to do it. You can change the way people respond to you by finding out how others view you. Learn to watch for and read responses from those around you.

The Handshake

Let's talk about one of the most important and underestimated gestures you make when greeting others: *the handshake*. As we discussed earlier, first—and lasting—impressions are formed in only seconds, and one impression is based on the way you shake hands. Remember that a handshake is the only physical contact we usually have with someone in business and most interactions begin and end with that gesture.

Just because you've been offering your hand and shaking with others does not guarantee you've been making the right kind of impression. It seems as though men were taught at an early age to shake "like a man" and many women were never even taught to shake hands at all.

There are many misconceptions surrounding the handshake. Many men think they ought to wait for a woman to offer her hand before offering theirs. There is no need to wait, either party can offer their hand first. It's an act of friendliness and acceptance of the other person. I often ask men if they think they should shake differently with women than they do with other men and the majority of men think they should. When I ask them why, it is usually because they think women have petite hands and they think they might be too rough if they shake too hard. This is simply not true. Gender need not be an issue when it comes to handshakes.

You can pull off the ideal handshake by doing the following:

- Step forward

- Make eye contact

- Smile

- Try to smoothly match the web of your hand with that of the person you're greeting

- Give as much of your hand as possible in a firm, confident grasp

- Hold just for a moment or two and then release

- Grasp the hand firmly (without crushing), squeeze once, pump up and down twice, and then let go

- Don't grasp the other person's hand and elbow with both of your hands (Though many people do this, it can come across as either warm or patronizing. You don't want to risk overpowering someone on your first meeting.)

- Offer men and women an equally firm handshake

- Always extend your hand to those you greet (a handshake is a friendly gesture that shows you are eager to be with this person.)

Be generous with your handshake: it's a good way of creating a link with another person and helping you assess people. So shake hands often and do it in a firm, warm and gracious way. Offer your hand when:

- Being introduced or saying hello.

- Leaving or saying good-bye.

- Greeting someone from your business, company or organization, or a client or customer, when you run into them outside that context.

- Greeting others you know and have run into unexpectedly.

When in doubt about whether a handshake is appropriate, it's better to offer your hand than not. Again, that handshake creates the only *physical business connection* we have with another person. Shaking hands warms the communication, increases the potential for a successful exchange and lets you subtly begin sizing up that other person.

Your Stance

It's a fine line—don't slouch, but don't stand too rigidly, either. The slouch conveys boredom, lack of confidence or laziness. The rigid stance makes you appear uncomfortable, formal or otherwise ill-at-ease. You're not a soldier and you're not a scarecrow. Develop an upright but natural stance.

Watch yourself in a mirror. Or, look at yourself in pictures or on video. Do you like or reject what you see? Videos are a way to view ourselves as others do. Let someone videotape you in several different activities. Let that person tape you as long as is needed to capture you in a relaxed way (not straightening up unnaturally for the camera) and in sitting, standing and moving activities. Now sit down and watch. Analyze what you see. Watching your natural posture might give you clues to ways you can correct how you hold yourself. Often, simply remembering to sit up straight during the day, with your head high and your shoulders back, is all you need to do to look, and feel, more energetic and professional. Looking at yourself honestly is the best way to make effective, necessary changes.

Your Movements

What happens when you're standing in the grocery store and you can't decide if you want plain or flavored coffee? You stand there looking at both products. You put your hand to your mouth, squint your eyes and frown in concentration. Your body slumps a bit. You move first toward one product, then reach for the other. What does all of this convey? Indecision!

Smooth, well-paced movements immediately say, "I know what I want and where to go to get it; in fact, I'm on my way there now." Graceful, non-hesitant movements, combined with good, upright posture, say it all in one, powerful nonverbal cue: "I'm confident, knowledgeable and capable."

Early in my speaking career, I decided to videotape myself as a way of improving my presentations. Though I had been receiving excellent evaluations, I found that it was still scary to see myself on tape. I put off watching it for a week.

As it turned out, watching that tape was one of the most important and powerful steps I've ever taken as a professional speaker. I noticed things I didn't like, of course, but I also saw things I did like. After watching the tape, I didn't need to hide from myself any longer and I had some great ideas about aspects of my presentation I could change to improve my style.

Ask someone you trust to videotape you working at your desk, talking on the telephone and standing in front of a group of people making a presentation. Watch how you move. Try watching without sound. You'll be able to tell exactly how you were feeling in any videotaped situation by your body movements. Hesitant? Confident? Bold? It will be right there for you to name. Turn on a television show and watch it without sound to see how easy it is to tell who's the good guy, who's the bad guy, who's sad, who's angry, etc.

You want fluid, natural movements that are well paced, neither too fast nor too slow. Think of someone who has no sense of urgency, whose pace is overly relaxed. You'd probably decide that this person is lazy, unwell or not very bright. Imagine someone who is always in a hurry, dropping things, apologizing, never composed. You'd probably think he or she is unprepared, disorganized or having a bad day. All negatives. Something as simple as pacing your movements can convey either positive or negative messages about you. You can develop fluid body movements by simply *being aware* of how you move. Catch yourself when you're moving too fast, too slow, or with hesitancy.

Your stance also conveys a great deal about you. Even though you're standing or sitting still, the way you hold your body while you're stationary says something about your presence in that business interaction or meeting. For example, do you shift your weight from foot to foot or put all your weight on one foot while standing? Do you lean back in your chair when sitting? Do you shuffle your feet back and forth, cross and uncross your legs, or make other repetitive movements?

All of these habits take away from the image you want. Holding your body still and upright conveys: "I'm interested in what you have to say," "I'm in control," and "I know exactly what I'm going to do with the information you're imparting to me at this moment."

While upright, stand solidly with your weight evenly distributed on both feet. Don't sway back and forth. Keep your shoulders back, spine straight. When sitting, lean forward a bit to prevent rounding your back by allowing your lower back to rest against the chair. Keep your feet flat on the floor with one foot just ahead of the other. Keep your hands and body in an open position: you'll appear positive and approachable. Practice these sitting and standing stances until you find yourself naturally assuming these positions at all times.

Personal Space: Close Encounters of the Worst (and Best) Kind!

Everyone has an unconscious but powerful inner sense of personal boundaries. Generally, most of us are comfortable with another person when separated by at least three feet. This general rule about personal-space distance varies from person to person and culture to culture. The key thing to remember is that invading someone's personal space will make him or her feel threatened and uncomfortable.

When with someone you don't know at all, keep at least an arm's length between you; a distance of three feet or more is generally reserved for strangers or those you don't know well. By controlling the distance, you can control the encounter by making people feel more or less comfortable. We tend to have less touching and greater distance in North American culture, while other cultures might be more intimate.

Nino, a Russian foreign exchange student, told me that one of the most difficult things for her to adjust to during the year she spent in the U.S. was the lack of kissing and hugging. In her country, it's customary to hug and kiss on both cheeks when greeting anyone. In the U.S., touching or other displays of affection aren't a part of most interpersonal interactions, unless they occur within an intimate relationship.

Each culture observes varying degrees of touch and personal space boundaries. In some European cultures, if you don't stand close enough to smell the breath of the person you're talking with, you might offend him or her. By contrast, North Americans tend to back away from close encounters and feel threatened when our boundaries are invaded. An example that illustrates North American personal space considerations is an elevator encounter. We have this unwritten rule that if somebody is in the elevator and another person gets on, we automatically stand away from that person, not side by side. We go to the other end of the elevator because that gives us the space and distance we need to feel comfortable. *The key is to observe comfort—theirs and yours!*

Vocal And Verbal

Your Voice

An associate, Joan, had just started her career as a motivational speaker when we were invited to share the platform at a conference. As she got up to speak, overwhelmed by the crowd, young and inexperienced, she wasn't quite sure how to begin. Standing center stage, looking out at the audience, she shrugged her shoulders, raised her eyebrows and merely opened with a high-pitched "H-i-i-i?" Joan knew the minute she did it she had made a mistake. She struggled to get the audience back on track.

The minute you open your mouth to speak, your sound, volume and pitch all play together to create a message. Know how you want to sound and see to it that you sound just that way!

As a speaker, my voice is my business. When I was preparing to tape my second video, I was struggling with hoarseness. Because the taping was just two weeks away, I went to a doctor specializing in ear, nose, and throat medicine. After examining me, he told me I had nodules on my vocal chords formed from years of misusing them. He referred me to a speech pathologist where I first learned to rest my voice (no talking for three days) to get it back for my video taping. I continued to work with my speech pathologist for a year to learn correct breathing, posture, and delivery skills.

How do *you* sound? To find out, record yourself. Grab a tape recorder, pop a tape in and record yourself. Capture yourself everywhere—on the phone, in your own office, at lunch. Considering asking permission to tape a meeting of a group you belong to so you can hear yourself as you respond to others. Then listen. You'll find, perhaps much to your amazement, that you don't sound at all like yourself! Why? Because ears, placed at the side of the head, pick up the sound of your own voice only peripherally—you never hear yourself directly. The result? How you sound to yourself and how you sound to others are *very* different.

People who have unique and pleasing voice quality can market their voices and sometimes a voice becomes a trademark. Think of James Earl Jones. His deep, soothing voice has been his trademark. And what about Demi Moore? You can recognize her voice easily and she is often described by the sound of her voice. Melanie Griffith is another example of an actress who is well known for her voice. She has continued to play many similar roles, possibly because her voice limits her. Many women speak in a pitch higher than they need to and could enhance their sound and credibility by lowering their pitch a bit.

How You Sound to Others

When you listen to yourself on tape, look for the following (circle yes or no).

- **Diction.** Do you pronounce letters and sounds correctly?   Yes/No

- **Clarity.** Do you speak clearly without mumbling?
                                                        Yes/No

- **Grammar.** Do you speak grammatically?   Yes/No

- **Slang.** Do you avoid as much as possible using slang, jargon or swear words?   Yes/No

- **Repetitive speech.** Do you speak clearly and directly without clearing your throat, coughing repeatedly, or using phrases such as, "you know," "um," or "ah," etc.?   Yes/No

- **Inflection.** Do you vary your tone and strive to sound animated and interested?   Yes/No

- **Volume.** Do you speak audibly but not too loudly?
                                                        Yes/No

- **Pitch.** Do you speak with a soothing, mellow pitch, neither too low nor too high, with no nasal, rough or squeaky tones? Yes/No

- **Listening.** Do you listen, without interrupting, more than you talk? Yes/No

  Based on the "no" answers you circled in this checklist, these are the areas on which you need to work.
  1. _____
  2. _____
  3. _____

Once you've identified how you sound to others, you can take some simple steps to improve your voice. First, think about how you'd like to sound to others. Most of us want to sound confident, assertive, in control, sure of ourselves and our needs.

If you think you need to, consult with voice experts to help you identify problems and work to develop or even change your speaking voice and style. For example, a communications specialist can help you improve your public speaking. A professional media consultant can help with television, film, video, radio and press conference appearances or speaking opportunities. And a speech pathologist can help with specific speech or voice problems.

To summarize, this is what you want to achieve in voice quality:

1. Good diction, so you're easy to understand in all speaking situations, in public or one-on-one.

2. Warmth and strength to show a sense of competence and confidence.

3. Expression through varying pitch and rhythm to convey your interest, energy and grasp of the subject matter.

4. Modulation in volume and rate of speech so you're not speaking too loudly, softly, rapidly or slowly.

5. Grammatical language and appropriate vocabulary conveying your knowledge and competence. Remember that an extensive vocabulary and complex sentences might be difficult for some of your listeners to follow. In fact, instead of sounding intelligent and knowledgeable, you could come off as pompous, perhaps even arrogant.

6. Avoidance of repetitive words, phrases, or other vocal habits that diminish your presence by making you appear nervous or otherwise dreary. Here is a list of words and phrases to watch for and the unflattering messages they convey:

Word/Phrase	Message Conveyed
You always/never/only/ever	blaming, exaggeration
Everybody or anybody	grandiosity, refusal to take personal responsibility
I don't know/care…	no ownership, no power, lightweight
It doesn't matter…	no conviction, not willing to take a stand
You know/Okay?/I mean/ Um/ Ah	uncertainty, nervous filler
Yup/Nope/Uh-huh/Yeah	Lack of sophistication

7. Proper intonation, where your voice drops at the end of each sentence. A new, and unfortunate, trend in speech is the raised intonation at the end of every sentence. The net effect is that each sentence sounds like a question: "I'll attend the meeting? But I can't stay long? So could you take notes for me?" If you haven't heard this yet, listen more closely to general conversation—you're apt to hear it soon. When you do, train your ear to find such intonation distasteful and remind yourself not to do it. Making a statement that sounds like you're asking a question takes away power by making you appear to be seeking approval.

Your Gestures

While we're on the subject of speaking, notice the gestures you make while you speak. Whether at the lectern delivering a formal speech, participating in a meeting, or at lunch with business associates, become aware of what your hands are doing. Nervous hand gestures or other repetitive movements can be very distracting to an audience of one or two hundred. No need to have the boss or your best customer ducking your fork while you emphasize your point.

On the other hand, when used in moderation, gestures can add impact to what you say. Have a home base like a conference table or desk upon which to rest your hands until you wish to gesture to emphasize a point.

Here are four rules about hands:

1. Don't put your hands in your pockets and keep them there indefinitely.

2. Find the median point in hand gestures: don't use them too much, but don't nail them to your sides,

either. It's important to use hand gestures to emphasize a point now and then.

3. Keep your hands to yourself! Other than the hand-
    shake, don't touch another person without his or her
    permission. Any touching can be interpreted, how-
    ever subconsciously, as an unwanted intrusion on
    personal space.

4. Keep your hands away from your face. Don't fuss
    with your glasses, play with your hair or put your
    hands up to your mouth: these gestures distract and
    prevent others from seeing your facial expressions.

Some gestures can add impact and help convey your message; some gestures will distract your audience. Here's a list of
gestures that convey nervousness.

- Biting fingernails

- Twisting rings

- Playing with hair

- Rubbing your nose or your ear

- Stroking your body

- Doodling excessively

- Tapping your fingers

- Fidgeting

Acceptable gestures conveying a positive or helpful message
include the following.

- Nodding in agreement

- Making consistent eye contact

- Tilting your head slightly to show interest

- Smiling

- Clasping your hands in front of you

- Placing your hands together in a pyramid or steeple formation

- Using broad, sweeping but controlled gestures

- Resting your chin on your hand or fingers (thought position)

- Making strong, specific movements

- Resting your open hands on a table

- Holding a pen without playing with it

Which Expressions Do You Use?

Facial expressions convey a great deal about you and your response to the person, situation or meeting in which you're involved. Unfortunately, we can't see ourselves and so are often unaware of what expression is on our face. And that *is* unfortunate, because others can see us and are picking up messages from our faces.

1. Circle words on the right that best show what you think these facial expressions convey.

   No expression:
       shy   neutral   bored   disinterested

Smile:
    deceptive   friendly   happy   outgoing

Tight, set lips:
    rigid   cautious   uptight   confused

Squinted eyes:
    thinking   tired   worried   unsure

Raised eyebrows:
    surprised   flirtatious   angry   interested

You'll find that the words on the left have several possible meanings. The message? Be careful about what your facial expressions are conveying to others and vary your expressions accordingly.

2.   How would you rate your facial expressiveness?

__ **Good.** I vary my facial expressions, smile frequently and control my expressions when necessary to mask true feelings. (For example, you are in a meeting and someone makes a comment you consider to be ridiculous. Your inclination may be to laugh, roll your eyes or snicker, but instead you remain expressionless. Or perhaps you've just met with a customer who is demanding and irritating. You may feel tense and frustrated, yet you know you need to keep smiling and act in a pleasant manner without showing your irritation.)

__ **Fair.** I have an open, confident expression, but I'm frequently not aware of what I'm conveying through my facial expression. (There are times when a neutral expression is important and the key is knowing/recognizing those times. Perhaps you have confidential information that someone wants from you or people are talking about a subject in which you don't wish to get involved. A neutral expression can be an advantage in some situations.)

___ **Needs work.** I'm not aware of what my facial expressions convey. (Perhaps people misunderstand you. You can't figure out why you need to defend what you say or you feel people don't take you seriously. It could be that your facial expression contradicts your words and causes confusion to your listener.)

3. Which specific areas do you need to improve?

___ Smile: not smiling or smiling too much.

___ Neutral expression: not showing any expression at all, which can convey a lack of interest, even hostility.

___ Unvaried expression: forgetting to show response to people via expression.

___ Tight, set lips, squinted eyes or raised eyebrows: an convey anger, distrust or confusion.

4. These are the specific areas of facial expressiveness that I will work on:

_____

_____

_____

Start to become more aware of your expressions by thinking about them. Ask people for clarification if you sense a lack of understanding. Sit or stand in front of a mirror and practice. Try making different facial expressions. Look happy, then sad, then frustrated. I always enjoy watching participants practice different facial expressions in my workshops. I have everyone select a partner. First I ask them to make eye contact and just look at each other. It never fails, they all break out into laughter. So we try again and again. I tell them to listen to the words I speak and to respond to them without using words, to just show a reaction with their face. I usually start by telling them to show anger. Some pout, others squint their eyes and eventually everyone breaks into laughter. In a group of 20 people I will see 20 different interpretations of each emotion I mention. Everyone perceives and displays emotions differently. It takes a lot of practice to be able to read the nonverbal signs of others effectively. Sometimes we think of a person as cold or aloof when in fact they are uneasy or shy. It takes more than a glance to understand someone, but by becoming more observant of others you will increase your ability to read more accurately the messages they send.

Maintaining eye contact is another important aspect of non-verbal communication. Avoiding eye contact, or shifting, darting eyes can send several negative messages: I'm not interested, I'm bored, I have something else to do, I don't like you, I don't like what you're saying, etc. *Maintain direct eye contact up to 90 percent of the time.* Focus on the person you're talking to, by looking at the eyes, mouth, or other facial area close to the eyes.

Many people have a fear of addressing a large group. If speaking in front of others is part of your job, the same principles will apply. Look over your audience and seek out a few friendly faces and make contact with them. Don't overdo it or you may make someone feel uncomfortable. Make contact and hold the glance five seconds before you move on. If you don't look at people you won't connect with them. Though you may feel self conscious in front of people, try to appear relaxed and be yourself. I have read many books on making presentations and sought the advice of experts in an attempt to improve my speaking skills. Yet some of the techniques I would try felt unnatural. One coach told me to stand still. Yet when I speak in front of a group, my adrenaline starts pumping and I need to walk around and use my energy efficiently. When I stood still, I didn't communicate as effectively. If I were to tell someone who wanted and needed to stand behind a lectern to get out and pace back and forth, it would be unnatural for them. We all need to be ourselves first and then do what we can to add to our overall presentation. Most of the ideas and principles in this book will be just as effective one on one as they are in front of a large group.

Verbal and Nonverbal Cues That Say It All

The image you convey can and should be controlled by you at all times. Once you know the image you want to project, make sure that all your verbal and nonverbal cues are communicating that image.

For example, control the length and type of verbal exchange you have with others by asking either open- or close-ended questions. Open-ended questions invite a longer, more detailed response: "How did you develop that particular approach to the marketing problem?" Or, "How did you come up with that quantity?" A close-ended question asks for a specific response that is fast and to-the-point: "What quantity do you need?" or "Can you meet next week?"

You can also control your verbal cues to indicate endings. Meetings, phone conversations or other interactions are often difficult for many of us to end. Knowing how to swiftly and smoothly end a conversation is a verbal skill you can use to control your time and reach your goals more effectively. Verbal cues include the actual words, "I have to go to a meeting now." or words that imply an ending, "I'll call you tomorrow to report status on this."

Nonverbal cues used to end in-person interactions can be as effective as words. For example, standing up and reaching out your hand to shake the other person's hand is a sure way to end a meeting. Gathering up papers on the conference room table in front of you and placing them in your briefcase, or sliding your coat on are other nonverbal ways of indicating that you are moving on to your next task.

Points to Remember

1. Sit and stand with upright posture.

2. Move with grace and confidence.

3. Control your hand and other gestures.

4. Use a vocabulary that communicates clearly; avoiding complex words or sentences in an attempt to impress your audience.

5. Listen to yourself and work with your voice to control its warmth, strength and resonance.

Questions and Answers:
Movement/Body Language/Nonverbal Communication

At the beginning of this chapter, you tested your understanding of nonverbal communication. After reading through the chapter, do you know some things you didn't know before? Compare your answers to these.

1. An effective handshake should involve at least four to five pumps up and down.

   FALSE.
   Short, sweet and to the point with one to three pumps maximum is best. Holding someone's hand too long is also not a good idea, doing that often makes others feel uncomfortable.

2. Smiling can make you appear friendly or influential.

    TRUE.
    A smile can make you appear friendly, approachable and influential. A smile is a valuable asset. It puts others at ease. The least expensive gift you can share with another is a smile.

3. Never look someone directly in the eyes—you risk being threatening or invading personal space.

    FALSE.
    Eye contact is essential to good communication. When you avoid eye contact you avoid connection. You don't want to have a stare-down, but it's a good idea to maintain eye contact about 90 percent of the time when conversing. It's natural to look away to collect your thoughts, but if more time than that is spent looking away, your message might indicate disinterest, insecurity or insincerity. If you find it hard to look at the eyes, make "face contact" by looking somewhere on the face.

4. Men should shake hands more gently with women than with other men.

    FALSE.
    Gender shouldn't be a consideration when offering your hand or determining how to shake hands. Handshakes in business have become universal. The type of handshake you give sends a message to those with whom you shake hands. A firm connecting shake rates well among men and women.

5. Showing no expression can make you appear hostile or uninterested.

   TRUE.
   Although some believe a neutral face is safest in business, it can have a negative effect. It's important to show human qualities: empathy, compassion, care and concern. Vary the expressions you use.

6. You will be perceived as more friendly and approachable when your body language is open (uncrossed arms and legs, directly facing the person you are talking with, pleasant facial expression, etc.).

   TRUE.
   Closed body language—crossed arms, folded hands, etc.— conveys hostility and distrust. Hands that are out of pockets and arms that hang relaxed and loose at your side communicate friendliness and openness to others' point of view.

7. Nervous gestures (hair twisting, finger tapping, etc.) are distracting to your message.

   TRUE.
   Any gesture repeated is likely to be noticed and irritating. In fact, such habits can overshadow anything you say because it becomes the focus of others' attention. Controlled gestures put you in a better position and add impact to what you say.

8. Sitting or standing up straight and holding your head high can increase your energy level.

TRUE.
It's difficult to be enthusiastic and energetic while shuffling your feet and slouching. Simply changing your posture can be an instant pick-me-up by increasing blood flow to your body and improving your attitude.

9. Nonverbal body language often tells the truth, despite verbal communication.

TRUE.
We might find it easy to sell a story verbally to someone, but our bodies have a much more difficult time with deception. Watch and learn from other people. Learn to read their signals.

The Attitude Advantage

Performance Counts, But So Does Your Attitude

Throughout this book, we identify many areas in which your professionalism is displayed. The kind of impression you make, the way you carry yourself, your tone of voice, and the clothes you wear all reflect how you feel about yourself. In the first chapter, you were introduced to the five components of your professional image:

Impression

Movement

Attitude

Grooming

Etiquette

It is essential to focus on each one of the five components equally because they all work together to help convey a positive and professional image. It's not enough to dress well and look great, you need to carry yourself with confidence and put a smile on your face too.

Several years ago, I presented a workshop to the sales associates of a temporary help agency. During the session I noticed a well-dressed male participant who was listening intently to everything I had to say as he diligently took notes. After the session was over he came up to me and told me that he agreed with the principles I was teaching and that he too, believed appearance was critical to success. It was obvious that he did. He stood about six feet tall and had a large, muscular build. He had dark black hair, which was slicked back off his face, small features, and wore a very expensive suit with a sharp tie, cuff links, and a pocket square. The problem he was having, he said, was that since he had become a sales manager, he was getting feedback from customers that they found him aloof and uncaring. He was very concerned because he did care about his clients and felt his business was suffering as a result of this false perception. I looked at him and responded with the first thought that came into my mind. "Do you ever smile?" I asked. He looked me straight in the eyes and without any expression replied, "Well, I don't know. I take my work very seriously and I'm not the type to make small talk to get too personal with my clients. I prefer to get right down to business."

After talking with him for just a few minutes, I concluded that the reason his clients found him uncaring and aloof was probably because of his attitude and his own discomfort with relating to his clients as people. Sure he looked good, but good looks simply aren't enough. Each image component needs to be working well in order to achieve the type of professional image you need to gain the edge. If you do everything right—look good, carry yourself well, master the latest rules of etiquette, but have a bad attitude, you ruin the whole effect.

Your attitude is contagious to others. You can decide and control how you react to things that happen to you. There are some people who complain about everything and are negative, miserable people. There are others who always seem optimistic and happy. Either one can drive you crazy if taken to an extreme, but given the choice, would you rather be around upbeat, energetic people or people who are miserable and whine about everything?

When I decided to leave the university and go into sales, many skeptics told me it was a bad idea. After all, I didn't have a degree nor any relevant job experience. Cautious and concerned people told me I'd never get a job with so few qualifications, but I knew better. I knew I could relate well with people and knew that sales was something I would be good at. I sent out résumés and responded to ads and was called in for interviews. I began to hear some of the same things over and over. "You don't have the qualifications we want, but I think you have what it takes to be in sales." "You've got enthusiasm and confidence." The very qualities that were attractive to the people I interviewed with are the qualities that many highly qualified job candidates were without. I was finally given a chance with a company and began my career in sales. To this day, I believe that the reason I was hired and the reason I was successful was because of my attitude. What else could it be? I didn't have the qualifications my employer sought, but I had drive and enthusiasm.

There are many people who have impressive résumés, but they have self doubt, lack ambition and initiative and don't relate well to people. *The attitude you convey makes the difference.*

To help you evaluate your own attitude and image, read through the following list of descriptive words and circle any words that you believe describe you.

creative	shy	fun	independent
diplomatic	extroverted	sophisticated	witty
dignified	satisfied	self-reliant	polished
calm	arrogant	confident	influential
distinctive	professional	controlled	successful
meek	cautious	respectful	impatient
wholesome	efficient	determined	reserved
self-centered	casual	masculine	enthusiastic
approachable	intellectual	original	delicate
innocent	blending	classic	savvy
dramatic	controlling	flirtatious	active
authoritative	restrained	severe	unique
feminine	disciplined	cold	naive
gentle	friendly	gracious	fashionable
sarcastic	aggressive	elegant	persuasive
humble	attractive	stubborn	bold
loyal	negative	charming	open minded
cheerful	precise	competitive	considerate
harmonious	inspiring	obedient	sociable
receptive	cordial	daring	soft spoken
convincing	tolerant	persistent	optimistic
positive	accurate	restless	polite
peaceful	tough	distant	kind
outspoken	assertive	introverted	

Now take a look at the words you have circled and put a star by the words you think are assets. Then look through the list again and put a check mark by any word you believe is a detriment or might hold you back from achieving your goals. Next, read through the following list of the same words, but this time think about the characteristics of successful people and circle all of the words that you believe are essential for success or that describe someone who is successful.

creative	shy	fun	independent
diplomatic	extroverted	sophisticated	witty
dignified	satisfied	self-reliant	polished
calm	arrogant	confident	influential
distinctive	professional	controlled	successful
meek	cautious	respectful	impatient
wholesome	efficient	determined	reserved
self-centered	casual	masculine	enthusiastic
approachable	intellectual	original	delicate
innocent	blending	classic	savvy
dramatic	controlling	flirtatious	active
authoritative	restrained	severe	unique
feminine	disciplined	cold	naive
gentle	friendly	gracious	fashionable
sarcastic	aggressive	elegant	persuasive
humble	attractive	stubborn	bold
loyal	negative	charming	open minded
cheerful	precise	competitive	considerate
harmonious	inspiring	obedient	sociable
receptive	cordial	daring	soft spoken
convincing	tolerant	persistent	optimistic
positive	accurate	restless	polite
peaceful	tough	distant	kind
outspoken	assertive	introverted	

Look at the words you circled that describe yourself and those that describe a successful person. What characteristics do you believe are necessary to be successful (the ones you circled in the second list) that you don't see in yourself? What do you need to do to make the characteristics you see yourself possessing (the first list) coincide with the traits you believe successful people have (the second list)? Read through the words you circled on the second list again and put a star by three traits you will work on. The answers to what you need to do in order to gain the edge are right before your eyes in this exercise. Identifying and focusing on the traits you need to have is essential to gaining the edge.

Your attitude is evident in everything you do. Following are some of the most important aspects of a successful, professional attitude and manner in business.

Respect Others

How you treat others is a reflection of how you value them. Perhaps the problems surrounding gender issues, diversity and harassment would be eliminated if everyone lived with respect for others and their differences. Diversity makes the workplace a place of learning. Your respect for others is visible in many ways.

- Do you keep a comfortable distance when speaking with someone rather than invading their personal space?

- Do you respect an individual's title or rank by addressing them in a formal way?

- Do you respect their time when meeting with them or speaking on the telephone?

- Do you listen to what others have to say without correcting or interrupting?

By respecting others you earn respect in return.

Use "Please" and "Thank You"

Little things make a big difference. A simple "please" attached to a request, or a "thank you" when someone has done something for you, can make all the difference in the world. Being courteous towards others helps make people feel valued. It is the simplest way to motivate others and gain cooperation. In most cases, you can gain cooperation better by "asking" rather than "telling." Once someone does something for you, it is important to show your appreciation with a word of thanks.

Be on Time

Due to circumstances beyond your control, you may find yourself, on occasion, falling behind schedule. Unfortunately, being late for one meeting in the morning can have a "domino effect" that ripples through the rest of your day. Consistent lateness can be interpreted as being negligent, careless or disrespectful. It can make you appear disorganized, unprofessional or out of control. Avoid scheduling yourself too tightly. Plan for traffic delays, interruptions, and last-minute problems. *The length of time you keep someone waiting is often proportionate to the value you place on them.*

Speak Positively

Speak positively about your job, your organization, and your co-workers. Badmouthing other people can often backfire. Even if you do succeed in making others look bad, chances are even better that you'll succeed in making *yourself* look bad. *If you speak positively about others, they will be more likely to speak positively about you.*

Be Enthusiastic

Although some equate enthusiasm with nothing more than cheering at a football game, it is far more than that. Enthusiasm is an important business tool. Think of some encounters you have had when you were the customer. Think of the salespeople you have encountered who lacked enthusiasm, who seemed to be saying to themselves, "Hmmm...maybe if I ignore them they'll go away."

Compare those people with others who were happy, positive and enthusiastic about seeing you walk through the door. Then think about who is most likely to get your business next time. *Enthusiastic people are perceived as more promotable and successful.*

Take Pride in Everything You Do

As Mark Twain once said, "Always do right. This will surprise some people and astonish the rest." No matter what position you hold, your job is important. Each person is essential to their organization's overall success. Remember, no organization would accomplish much without all of the hard-working employees who support it. Work each day with energy and purpose. Whatever you do, give it your best. Take pride in your work. *A job worth doing is a job worth doing well enough so you can be proud of it.*

Smile

As discussed in Chapter Two, a smile can make you appear friendly, helpful and positive. Smiling is an important part of doing business. Your facial expressions speak for you before you have a chance to speak for yourself. Most people would rather be around someone who is smiling and pleasant. A smile is the fastest way there is to build rapport and acknowledge someone and their ideas. It takes 74 muscles to frown, and only 14 to smile.

Believe in Yourself

Be your own best advocate. If you don't believe in yourself, why should anyone else? You are your best salesperson, so sell your strengths, not your limitations. Don't tear yourself down in front of other people. Be honest about your shortcomings, but never stop believing in your unlimited potential. *You can achieve almost anything you want if you want it bad enough.*

Bring Out the Best in Others

When you make others feel good about themselves, they will feel good about you. Offering a sincere compliment is one way to make others feel good, and accepting a compliment graciously is important too. Some people withhold kind remarks because they believe it gives the other person too much power. The opposite is true. When you give of yourself to someone and make them feel good, they will think highly of you.

Can you think of someone you enjoy being around? The type of person who lights up a room and has the ability to lift your spirits? Can you think of someone who has the opposite effect? They are negative and depressing to be around, and you're usually drained after spending time with them? What effect do you have on others? Do you bring out the best in people? *Bring out the best in others and you'll bring out the best in yourself.*

Enjoy The Work You Do

It will much easier for you to maintain a positive, enthusiastic attitude if you enjoy the work you do. If you find yourself dreading the thought of going to work each day, consider making a change to something you will enjoy. Over your life, if you work full-time, you will spend more time at work than any other activity. You may as well make the most of it.

Try to think of your work as more than just "doing a job." Think about the contributions you can make and the positive effects you can have on other people. No matter what your chosen profession is, there is a way to add meaning to what you do.

Many people grow both professionally *and* personally as a result of the changes and challenges they encounter in their work. I have grown both mentally and emotionally as a result of my work. No matter what I've done, I've always had people tell me that what I do looks like so much "fun" or that I am so "lucky" to have a job like I do. When I hear this, I often question what exactly these people mean. Do they think what I do is easy, something I just fell into, given to me as a present?

When I started my business, it was anything but fun. It was lonely, I had no clients, no steady income and a product few people wanted. Believe me, I've had my moments when I wondered what I was doing, but deep inside I knew I was onto something and that I had a message people needed to hear. Even though it was a struggle some days to pull myself to the office, I managed to go and when I did I always enjoyed myself. If I didn't like what I did, I would have given up long ago. If you are unhappy in your chosen field, think about what you enjoy doing and think about making a change.

I was making great money as a sales-rep, but I was losing my zest for the job. The challenge wasn't there anymore. One of the hardest decisions for me was leaving, but I knew I had reached my potential in that business and needed to move on. I've had to travel long distances, take risks, go periods without making any money, and create demand for the product I was selling. Hard work, passion for what I do and determination have been crucial to my success. I am having fun and I do feel lucky, but these are things I believe I've created myself. Create your own happiness—do something you enjoy and have fun doing it!

Be the kind of person who creates positive, rather than negative energy. Remember, your overall success comes mainly from the way you handle yourself and others. *It all begins with the right attitude. Take control of yours.*

Points to Remember

1. Respect others.

2. Be on time.

3. Speak positively about others.

4. Be enthusiastic.

5. Take pride in everything you do.

6. Smile.

7. Believe in yourself.

8. Bring out the best in others.

9. Enjoy the work you do.

The Impact of Your Image: Your Appearance Counts

In this chapter, you'll focus on a more tangible element of your professional look: *clothing*. We'll look at daily professional business clothing. As was pointed out, clothing is one of the key factors in the first impression you make. Fair or not, we are often judged by our clothing before we even have a chance to open our mouths. Before discussing on-the-job clothing, check your knowledge about your business dress by taking the following true/false test.

Mark each statement true or false. Answers and explanations are at the end of the chapter.

1. Your clothing is the first thing that is noticed about you.   True/False

2. Shoes should always be the same color or darker than your hem color.   True/False

3. The fit of your clothing is more important than the style or quality.   True/False

4. Darker colors convey strength, power and authority.
    True/False

5. A solid, dark color will make you appear thinner.
    True/False

6. A suit is the most professional choice in business attire.
    True/False

Your Personal Style: Putting Your Look Together

I cannot stress enough how important it is to have a good idea of your personal style and a comfort zone within which you're willing to dress. Now you can make clothing decisions that not only fit your workplace, but also your personality and style. You don't have to be someone you're not to look and be successful.

Another true-life story illustrates this point:

Scott, a salesman in his first job out of college, wanted to be successful as well as look good. Early on, his talent and ability were noticed by his superiors and his peers. Heeding the advice of a fashion consultant, Scott wore European cut designer suits in unique colors and wild ties. Although he never felt totally comfortable dressed in such a trendy, fashion-conscious way, he believed the consultant knew more than he did.

When I met Scott, his eager attitude and willingness to please had gotten the best of him. "I work ten hours a day. I'm trying so hard and yet something isn't working—I just don't feel right dressed like this and I'd swear people are making comments about my clothes behind my back," Scott told me. "Maybe this isn't the business for me," he concluded.

Scott thought he might actually relate to his clients better if he took off his jacket, rolled up his sleeves and looked more like he was on their level. I encouraged him to speak with his supervisor and ask if it would be appropriate to dress more casually.

Scott did just that and ended up going to work every day wearing slacks, a button-down shirt and conservative tie. He felt much more comfortable—and confident. And his sales results began to reflect it.

The fashion consultant Scott worked with had failed to understand Scott's personal style and his workplace environment before recommending a successful look for him.

We all need to find the look that is right for us. What might be a great look for one person is not necessarily right or appropriate or even attractive for someone else. Staying true to your personal likes, dislikes, and comfort zone is essential in determining your personal style.

What Does Your Image Say About You?

Assessing Your Personal Style

1. What colors/types of clothing do you wear most often?

2. What colors/types of clothing do you feel best in?

3. What colors/types of clothing do you avoid? Why?

4. If you were to dress for an important meeting and were to select your "best" or favorite clothing, what would it be? (Describe in detail, including tie, watch, socks/hose and shoes.)

5. If you could select an acceptable, comfortable daily uniform, what would it be?

6. Think of someone in your field whom you consider to be particularly successful. What does that person wear? (Be as specific as possible.)

7. Which articles or styles of clothing would you *never* wear? Why not?

Review your response and think about what your clothing choices communicate about your attitude and intentions. Since it's a good idea to dress for the type of job you want to have, not necessarily the one you currently have, pay particular attention to #6—perhaps this person can serve as a role model.

What Image Does Your Clothing Convey?

It's important to think about what you wear and what your clothing communicates about you. When presenting workshops, I sometimes will ask the participants why they wore the clothing they have on that particular day, how they made their clothing decisions, and what they think their clothing communicates about them. I ask them, did you wear these clothes:

- Because they were clean?

- Because these clothes fit well?

- Because every Monday, this is what you wear?

- Because someone else picked it out for you?

- Because of the weather? You wanted to be warm or cool?

People often laugh because, odd as it may seem, most didn't give their clothing choices much thought prior to the moment I asked them about it. What you choose to wear says so much about you and how you feel about yourself. The style, color, and fit communicate your intentions, attitude, and level of professionalism. Remember, your clothing is one of the first things noticed, so you need to select styles that enhance your professionalism. Dress for the job or position you want to have—not the one you currently have. If you wish to be perceived as successful or ready for a promotion, you have to look successful and look ready! We'll cover clothing in more detail a bit later, but remember that a big part of your professional image is tied up in your attire.

What's In a Color?

Color presents a message of its own. While you might have your own color preferences in both dress and environment, it's important to understand the impact the colors you wear can have on others. Sometimes we subconsciously avoid people wearing a color we don't like—and, conversely, others may avoid us if we're wearing a color they dislike. You're less likely to trust or buy from someone dressed in a color which you— unaware of the situation—find threatening or unappealing. Communication can be disrupted when you are surrounded by colors to which you react poorly.

Companies invest considerable time and money in choosing the appropriate color schemes for their offices and their products. The color they choose must match the message they intend to send.

Color adds excitement and helps us express our style and taste in many areas of our lives. How appealing would a plain metal (colorless) car be to drive? How appetizing would gelatin be if all the flavors were clear?

In clothing, neutral, basic colors are always safe. You might stand out and be remembered, negatively, as the one in the bright orange suit, but rarely will you leave a negative impression for being dressed in navy blue or any basic color.

In general, lighter shades have been found to communicate a more approachable, non-threatening image, while darker colors communicate more authority and power. For example, to appear and feel more authoritative yet approachable, wear a dark suit (which says "authority") with a light blue or yellow shirt (a lighter, less threatening color). To appear and feel more authoritative, wear a white shirt. To appear and feel more calm, wear a color from the blue family. A blue suit is less intimidating than a black one.

In making public presentations, consider both your audience and the message you intend to deliver. When speaking and acting from a position of authority, *dress* authoritatively. In our culture, that means wear a dark suit, no exceptions. On the other hand, when you are meeting with others in a more conciliatory or advisory capacity, tone down your color scheme, so that your clients or customers feel comfortable, non threatened, and free to open up.

The key here, of course, is to *consider your audience*. When you're applying for a job, making an important client presentation, conducting a performance review of an employee, prosecuting an accused criminal, *defending* an accused criminal, making a sales call, waiting on customers in a department store: What message do you want to communicate? What image do you want to project?

You can use this information to *consciously* control the image you project. By taking a little time to think through the encounters you anticipate each day, you can use color to convey your intended message.

Color can also be used to enhance your silhouette and camouflage an imperfect physique. Since the eye is drawn to the lightest spot of the silhouette, it is important to place color strategically. A white shirt, for example, puts the focus on just the right area—the face. Light shoes or socks with dark slacks, however, will draw attention to your feet! Always wear the lightest colors next to the areas to which you want to draw attention.

A solid, dark color can make you look taller and thinner. A navy, charcoal gray or black suit with dark socks and shoes creates a smooth, monochromatic line and is thus more slimming than a light-colored suit or a sport coat and slacks in contrasting colors, such as navy and tan.

Following are some characteristics of colors. As you read through the list, pay attention to the colors you wear most often and what they communicate about you.

Characteristic	Colors
Assertive	black, dark gray, blue-red, navy
Creative/Artistic	mauve, yellow, white
Traditional/Classic	medium brown, taupe
Intuitive/Sensitive	indigo, periwinkle blue, purple
Friendly	peach, pale yellow, tan, grass green
Energetic	true red
Powerful	black
Approachable	peach, tan, pale and medium pink, coral, rust
Authoritative	charcoal gray, navy, black
Inventive/Soothing	teal, turquoise
Trustworthy/Organized	navy
Conservative	dark brown, medium gray
Sophisticated	burgundy, forest green, black, plum, brick red

Clothing matters in business. What you wear affects how you are perceived which, in turn, can affect your overall success. It would be nice if we were all noticed for our hard work or honorable intentions alone. But your appearance sends a strong message that precedes your chance to impress with good work.

Remember, less than 10 percent of your message comes from the words you speak. The visual conveys the rest.

When you show up for work each day, how you look reflects how you feel about yourself, your job, your customers, and your co-workers. Even on tired, slow days, it's important to put effort into your appearance and behavior. Others will always seek out the person who appears to be eager to help, knowledgeable, and conveys a positive attitude.

Fabric Sense: What Works Best

The best suit fabric to buy is wool. Wool suits may cost more, but they look good and last. A good wool suit will drape beautifully, resist wrinkling, breathe, clean well without showing wear and, in the long run, will last longer. It may cost more upfront, but it's worth the investment.

You can test the fabric in a suit by subjecting it to the "feel and wrinkle" test. First, try it on. How does it feel to you? If it's comfortable, it passes the "feel" part of the test. Then crumple or squeeze it. Let it go. Does the fabric retain the creases? The way it looks after crumpling is an indication of how it will look when you wear it. If it looks good after scrunching, it also sails by the "wrinkle" test. Darker colors show less wrinkling. Do the wrinkle test for outer fabrics like suits but also consider how it feels before making the purchase. *Remember: You're better off having fewer clothing items of better quality than a lot of cheap clothing.*

The Professional Look

When you think of professional dress, what comes to mind? For men, it's usually a suit and tie, but for women it's everything from a suit to a dress to a skirt and blouse to slacks. The media, retailers, and fashion magazines dictate their ideas about what professional dress should be but rarely do these mediums really pin down what works in business. Styles shown are often too tight, too short, or simply too fashion-conscious.

What works best in business is simple, well-tailored clothing. Because there is such a wide range of choices, it's often difficult to know what to wear. Here, in order of professional appearance, are good options for men and women. For women, the skirted suit is still considered the most professional over the pantsuit, though pantsuits are gaining in popularity. We'll discuss business casual styles in a different chapter.

Women: Most Professional Style in Order of Professionalism

(From most professional to most casual)

- Two-piece matching skirted suit.

- Skirt with jacket.

- Two-piece matching pantsuit.

- Business dress with jacket

- Business dress

- Skirt and blouse

- Slacks with jacket

- Slacks with blouse or sweater

- Jean skirt with vest

- Casual pants with casual shirt

- Jeans with shirt and jacket

- Spandex leggings with sweaters

- Walking shorts with top

- Running or jogging suit

- Jeans and sweatshirt

Men: Most Professional Style in Order of Professionalism

(From most professional to most casual)

- Two-piece matching suit

- Slacks with sport coat or blazer

- Shirt with tie and slacks

- Shirt with tie, sweater and slacks

- Shirt, no tie, slacks and jacket.

- Casual pants with casual shirt and jacket

- Casual short-sleeved shirt and casual pants

- Jeans with shirt and jacket

- Jeans with shirt or sweater

- Walking shorts with shirt

- Running or jogging suit

- Jeans and sweatshirt

For both men and women, choose good quality fabrics for all clothing. Although women have more clothing styles and options available to them, it's safest to limit those options to the same options men follow in the workplace. Short sleeves on men or women, even in summer, are not as sophisticated as long sleeves. I know what you're thinking about those hot summer days. It doesn't really make sense to dress in long sleeves, but be grateful for air conditioned buildings and, of course, be practical too.

You can upgrade your image and professionalism by wearing a jacket. A jacket communicates authority and completes your outfit. Invest in a good jacket that will mix with other items in your business wardrobe.

In all cases, stick to business dress and save your personal style touches for situations outside your work environment. When you look professional, your appearance shows you take pride in yourself and your work.

Smart Shopping With Your Budget in Mind

You can save some money when purchasing your initial wardrobe and in maintaining it each year by waiting for sales in good quality retail clothing stores, or shopping the discount and outlet stores. The key to doing this successfully, whether you're shopping the sales at your usual clothing store, or searching the racks at a discount store, is going in with a plan. *Know exactly what you need before you step foot in any store.*

Retail stores have sales several times a year, generally for spring, summer, fall and every holiday in between. If you choose to shop at these sales, go with list in hand so you buy only the items you need. That great bargain will only be good for you if you can use and wear it, not just because it is a "good deal. Check quality, color, size and fit before you decide to buy. If you've shopped around enough, you should have enough knowledge about fabric, labels and prices to know if what you're considering really is a bargain.

You can also find a clerk in the store to work with you. A clerk who knows you, can help you find what you're looking for when you're shopping and can call you when something you want goes on sale. You don't necessarily have to use a formal clothing consultant to do this. Just getting to know a clerk, seeking that person out whenever you shop in that store, and leaving your business card so he or she can let you know when particular items go on sale can save you both time and money.

Discount and outlet stores offer a good, sometimes even great, alternative to paying full price. You can find some great deals if you shop carefully. Some discount and outlet stores are better than others. Watch for quality, fit, correct size and low to reasonable price. Be careful about merchandise that may be in the "seconds" category that isn't marked that way. Inspect all discount and outlet merchandise for flaws; look for color flaws, snags, tears or miss-matched patterns. Check for poor sewing. Is one sleeve longer than the other? Does the jacket or pant leg hang funny? Are there puckers in shirt seams, lapels or jacket seams? Do the pants hang correctly from the pleat?

If the discount is substantial, if the clothing can be altered or fixed, and if it's still a value after your investment in tailoring, then consider buying it.

Fabric is one of the most important elements in determining the cost of a garment and how well it will wear. Following is a chart listing advantages and disadvantages of most commonly selected fabrics.

Fabric	Advantages	Disadvantages
Wool	• can be worn year round • resists wrinkling • suitable for any business occasion • long lasting • breathes well	• costs more up front • needs to be dry cleaned
Silk	• lightweight • more casual styles are available • comes in a variety of colors	• wrinkles easily • requires ironing or dry cleaning • usually expensive • spots and stains easily
Cotton	• breathes well • machine washable • reasonably priced • durable	• wrinkles easily • requires ironing • color can fade
Linen	• lightweight • reasonably priced	• wrinkles easily • color can fade • requires ironing or dry cleaning

How To Get the Most from Your Clothing Dollar Investment

When you have a special occasion such as a class reunion, wedding, etc., you might find yourself shopping for the right clothes for that particular event and, perhaps, spending a lot of money doing it. Yet, the one item you find might be worn only at that occasion or only a handful of times after.

We often place less importance on the clothing we wear to work, shuddering at the thought of spending a lot of money on something for everyday wear. Well, we all know the special feeling that comes with dressing for a special occasion. Why do we only allow ourselves to feel that just once in awhile? *Why not dress each day as if it were special?* That could affect our long-term goals!

Tips on What To Buy

- Buy quality. Spend more upfront to get that good, long-term investment.

- Buy high-quality fabrics, such as wool, silk or cotton.

- Pay attention to detail. Buy what looks good and fits well right down to the small touches.

- Buy clothing that is true to your personal style, that brings out your personality and helps you feel comfortable and at ease.

- Keep in mind the standards of your company, your clients, and your customers.

Effective Shopping Tips

- Look good when you shop. The better you look the better service and attention you're likely to get.

- Wear the shoes you intend to wear with the item you're looking to buy. It's hard to get a sense of how a suit or pair of slacks really look when you're wearing sneakers.

- When you're debating about whether a particular clothing item is too casual, apply this rule: it's better to be slightly overdressed than underdressed.

- Plan your shopping. Avoid impulse buying. Know exactly what you need before you enter a store.

- Shop on a week day when stores are less busy.

- Shop alone if you do best that way, or shop with someone you know who will help rather than hinder you.

- Shop when you're feeling good.

- Avoid major sales if you don't do well with crowds, want personal attention or tend to buy on impulse.

- Gain the support and help of a clerk to assist you both with shopping that particular day as well as in calling you if something you want goes on sale or comes in stock.

- Wear clothing that is easy to get in and out of so trying things on isn't a chore.

- Don't "shop until you drop." Take a break, go have lunch and avoid getting exhausted—you'll make better decisions and be more likely to stick to your plan when you're fresh.

Shopping for the clothing you need should be both fun and rewarding. If you have a plan before you go, you'll be more likely to come home with just the clothing you need.

Tailoring Tricks

So you've purchased a good quality jacket, skirt, suit or dress. That's not all there is to it. A perfectly good suit can look shabby, even obsolete, without attention to finer details addressed by a good tailor. Tailoring helps you pay attention to very fine details that might seem small, but are very important. These small details distinguish an average suit from a high quality one.

Here are some examples of the kinds of details to pay attention to in dresses, skirts and suits:

- Does it hang nicely?

- Is it even?

- Is it too long or too short?

- Does the sleeve length break at the wrist when your arms are hanging down?

- Do the seams/lines match?

- Are the buttons sewn tightly (but not too tightly) so they don't hang loose or fall off?

- Do the vents of the jacket lie flat?

- Does anything pull? Check the shoulders, chest and hips.

- Can you move freely? Lift your arms, bend and sit comfortably?

Here are some other factors to watch for in good tailoring.

- Linings should never show

- The color of the zipper should match the fabric color

- Seams should be smooth and well-finished, with no puckers in the fabric

- Shoulder pads should be invisible

- Snaps should be hidden

- Hem should hang straight and evenly

- Patterns should match at the seams

- Undergarments should never show (bra straps, button gaps, slips hanging below hem, etc.)

- Pants should break at the instep and cover the top of the shoe heel

- Skirts should be no shorter than 3" above the knee and no longer than the bottom of your calf

Little Things Make All the Difference

There are a host of little details, many which seem trivial in and of themselves, which can make or break even the most put-together professional ensemble. As an example, imagine yourself in this scenario:

You're making an important sales call on a potential customer. You've dressed carefully to "fit in" with the appearance norms of your customer's company. Your shoes are polished, your hair newly cut, you feel great. But as you leave your office, you realize you spilled something on your shirt or blouse at lunch. You don't have an extra shirt or blouse with you, and you haven't left enough time to make an emergency stop to buy a new one.

Remember, in face-to-face encounters, eyes meet eyes, then sweep down to the feet and back up to the face again. The spot on your garment will be noticed. What should you do? You probably will make an effective sales pitch and land the account, but this sort of detail does register with the observer as a negative. *When your image communicates something negative about you rather than positive, you've lost control of the message you want to get across.* When the details are wrong, your power and effectiveness are severely reduced.

Here's a story that illustrates how details can contradict, sometimes in very concrete, visible ways, the message we mean to convey.

A printing salesman recently called on me in my office. He came inside with his overshoes on and his tie flipped over his shoulder as if blown by the wind. As he stood there talking to me, all I could concentrate on was the marks his dirty overshoes were making on the carpet of my office, and how funny his tie looked. No matter what he had to say, these two things said it all—far louder than his words!

You can prevent as many things as possible by predicting or planning for them, but if something happens, always go forth with confidence, trying not to focus on the problem. It might be noticed, yes, but don't allow yourself to be irretrievably distracted or defeated by it. Keep your chin up and sell *yourself.*

In some cases, if the problem is an overwhelmingly obvious one (such as lunch spilled down your front), and is so noticeable that you would feel better drawing attention to it right off the bat, then do. Your "audience" will notice it anyway, but don't dwell on it; explain, apologize and then *move on.*

Points to Remember

Pay attention to details to maintain your professional edge:

1. Carry an emergency repair kit in your briefcase or car with an extra tie, cloth for wiping shoes, needle and thread, extra hose, toothbrush and toothpaste.

2. Keep an extra shirt or blouse, jacket, and pair of shoes in your office for emergencies.

3. Before you leave the house each morning, look at yourself, fully clothed, in a full-length mirror to get

the full effect of the image you project. Check your-self over head to toe: Shoes polished? Under-clothes invisible? Clothing lint-free?

4. Always buy quality, not quantity.

5. Hire a good tailor for a great fit.

6. Take advantage of discount stores and look for that great, good-quality bargain that you can use.

Questions and Answers:

Putting Your Look Together

1. Your clothing is the first thing that is noticed about you.

    TRUE.
    No matter what you wear, it sends a message that tells others a lot about you. Whether you're dressed in athletic wear, business attire, high fashion, or even a 60s-era look, you are sending a message about who you are, what you like, and what you dislike. Why do you wear the clothing you do? Because it feels like it's you.

2. Shoes should always be the same color or darker than your hem color.

    TRUE.
    Since the eyes are always drawn to the lightest spot of your silhouette, it is important to place color strategically. A white shirt, for example, puts the focus on just the right area— the face. Light shoes

with dark skirts, slacks or stockings, however, will draw attention to your feet! Always wear the lightest colors near your face.

3. The fit of your clothing is more important than the style or quality.

    TRUE.
    Even the most expensive garment won't look good if it's too tight, too loose, too short, too long, or doesn't fit well in other ways. Always make sure your clothing is tailored for you so the fit is good.

4. Darker colors convey strength and power.

    TRUE.
    Darker colors convey authority, which can sometimes mean that people will feel less comfortable communicating freely with you. Lighter colors, on the other hand, are more friendly and tend to make you appear approachable. Think about your objectives and the image you want to project when deciding what colors and tones to wear.

5. A solid, dark color will make you appear thinner.

    TRUE.
    A solid, dark color creates a smooth line and thus creates a thinner illusion. Anytime the line is broken, attention is drawn to the point where the "break" in the eye flow occurs. For example, a navy blazer and khaki slacks chops up a look while a solid colored suit presents a smooth line.

6. The most professional and formal choice in business attire is the two-piece matching suit.

    TRUE

    A business suit creates a polished look and communicates a serious attitude. You can never go wrong dressed in the business suit unless you work in an environment where a suit is inappropriate.

CHAPTER

Business Casual Days

Dressing for Business Casual

In the early 1990s, it was a trend; today it's the norm. Business casual has become business as usual. Whatever your company calls it—casual dress day, dress down day, or a relaxed dress code—business casual attire has made its mark on the workplace.

Circle true or false for each statement. Compare with answers and explanations at the end of the chapter.

1. The fit of your casual clothing is as important as the style and quality.　　　　　　　　　　True/False

2. The shoes you wear on casual dress day need not be in top condition.　　　　　　　　　　True/False

3. If you have clients coming to your facility for meetings on casual dress day, notify them in advance, so they can choose whether or not to dress casually as well.

　　　　　　　　　　True/False

4. If your company has a casual dress policy, you *must* dress casually on casual dress day.   True/False

5. It is not necessary to wear socks on casual dress day. True/False

6. On casual dress days, it is perfectly acceptable to save time by not washing your hair or taking a shower.
                                                                  True/False

7. Men need not shave on casual dress days.
                                                                  True/False

8. Sunglasses and hats, visors, or caps are all casually correct business attire.   True/False

Clothing is noticed right upfront—*before you even have a chance to speak.* Therefore, if one is to dress more casually on casual dress day, it's more important than ever to dress casually correct.

A casual day is not meant to be a day when you also become casual about your work, behavior, attitude, or overall appearance. It is a day to dress more casually while maintaining a high level of concern about your appearance.

Unfortunately, casual is often left to individual interpretation. Business casual means different things to different people if it's not defined. Some companies define what casual dress means. But many do not. Casual day is a new game with new rules. If your company has a casual dress policy, you'll have a good idea of what to wear. If not, here are some guidelines to help you put together the business casual look you prefer.

Universal Taboos of Casually Correct Dressing

Though each workplace environment has distinct differences, similarities exist across all workplace environments regarding what is considered appropriate and inappropriate ways of dressing.

No matter where you work, *casual dress days are not meant to be careless dress days.* Casual clothing appropriate for all workplace environments is always clean, pressed, mended, and fits well. Shoes are clean and polished, and always worn with socks.

You may be thinking, "All of this is obvious." That's what a client of mine thought too, until she found herself in the embarrassing position of actually sending her front-desk person home to change her clothes—because casual dress day to her meant dressing like Annie Oakley—right down to the leather, fringe, and ankle-length skirt—to greet corporate customers in a law office.

Across-the-board casual dress taboos include:

- **Ripped clothing.** Any clothing that is torn or has holes, no matter how fashionable, is not a becoming choice for work—ever.

- **Sweat suits.** Sweat suits and running suits are comfortable and perfect for exercising or washing the car. But they are too casual for any workplace.

- **Printed T-shirts and sweatshirts** and *any* shirt with potentially offensive slogans, pictures, or graphics are always casual *incorrect.*

- **Spandex and other tight clothing.** "Second skin" clothing has become a comfortable after hours option for both men and women. Whether flattering or unflattering, tight clothing draws attention to the body. In any workplace environment, this is a distraction and is inappropriate.

- **Baggy, extremely loose-fitting tops and pants.** These look just plain messy and unkempt. It's simply not professional to go to work looking like you're ready to clean the garage.

- **Short-shorts and cut-offs.** Short-shorts are fine for the beach, but when they're more than two to three inches above the knee, they're not acceptable for work.

- **Tank tops, muscle shirts, and halter tops.** Most sleeveless tops simply expose too much skin. On women, they also tend to reveal undergarments under the arm and at the shoulder. Many halter and tank tops are cut low enough to show cleavage—which is never appropriate in a business environment.

- **Sandals and dirty or worn-out shoes.** For health reasons as well as appearance, sandals shouldn't be worn to work. And, while comfort is an important factor in footwear, any shoes that are dirty or worn-out will not make it, even on casual dress day.

- **Sleepwear, lounge wear, or swimwear.** The names say it all. Sleepwear is for sleeping, lounge wear for lounging, and swimwear for swimming. None of these are business wear.

- **"Theme" clothing.** Costume looks such as Western wear, retro, and 50s or 60s vintage wear are too showy and theatrical for the workplace. Save it for the weekend.

Casual Defined

Many companies have implemented casual clothing days to improve morale, encourage creativity, or reduce stress. Casual dress days may be weekly or monthly, and may be defined simply as casual or a theme may be announced: wild tie day, T-shirt day, etc.

Though each company puts together its own individualized casual-dress policy, most will find a way to meet the employee needs while maintaining the company's professional image and competitive edge. Casual dress should be dictated by four simple rules.

1. Consider your customer.

2. A casual dress code doesn't mean no dress code.

3. Don't dress casually if you would prefer to wear traditional business attire.

4. Never forget, it's *business* first, *casual* second.

Here are some guidelines to consider regardless of your environment.

- **Selection:** Choose a style that flatters and will wear well.

- **Fit:** Check the fit of your clothing–sleeves should break at the wrist and pants at the instep. Don't wear clothing that is too big or too small. Consult a good tailor for alterations that can upgrade a look.

- **Color:** Though often overlooked, color plays an important role in an effective business casual look. Colors should be coordinated. Avoid unusual combinations that may make you appear unprofessional, such as bright orange, shocking pink or lime green. These may be trendy, but they're not neutral enough for most business environments.

- **Fabric:** Since fabric determines how well a garment will wear, select fabrics that resist wrinkling.

- **Clothing Care:** Care for you business casual clothing as you do for your other business clothing. Many cottons and linens will look better if you launder them professionally. If you clean them yourself, follow the laundering instructions for each article to insure that they look their best. Always make sure your clothing is clean and in good condition. Visible dirt or stains will be noticed, taking away from your look and professional edge.

- **Grooming:** Make sure you are well-groomed. A business casual day is not the time to forego your bathing, shaving, or hair styling habits. The same pride and care you take every day should also be taken on a business casual day.

What's Appropriate In Your Environment?

As you consider your business causal attire options, think about your *customers and clients.*

- What do *they* expect?

- How much face-to-face contact do you have with them?

- What business is your company in and what image do you need to maintain to be competitive in that business?

- Do they expect you to be dressed in a certain way to assure that your company is credible, trustworthy, and professional?

- Will casually dressed employees make them think you take your business casually? If so, will they take their business elsewhere?

Next, with your customers' needs and expectations in mind, define your *workplace environment*. In consulting with many companies nationally, I have found that most workplace environments fall into one (or more) of four broad categories.

- **Internal environments** are found in many industries and, characterized by the absence of face-to-face customer contact, tend to be the most casual.

- **External environments,** on the other hand, involve extensive public or customer contact, and thus must be especially sensitive to customer's expectations and desires—including expectations about how employees are dressed.

- **Traditional environments** are exactly what the name implies. They are traditionally conservative industries such as banking and finance in which status-linked dress codes are long established. Customer expectations also play a key role in this workplace environment.

- **Social environments** are business activities or occasions that occur in non-business settings such as meetings, conventions, seminars, company parties, picnics, or other informal gatherings. Because social events have become an integral part of conducting business today, it's important to wear appropriate attire.

Frequently employees in a company operate in more than one environment, depending on their job function and the amount of customer contact they have. In this case, function-specific dress may be a more practical and customer-centered option for you than trying to follow a universal policy.

Which environment applies to your organization? Consider these factors:

- geographic location

- amount of public or customer contact

- industry standards

- whether a service or production company

- physical labor involved in daily activity.

Business Casual for Each Environment

If you have visitors coming to your facility for meetings or on a business casual day, tell your clients or customers in advance. If they are coming to your company for meetings on a causal day, let them know so they may dress accordingly. If you know they will be dressed in traditional business attire, it's best to dress in the same manner.

Several basic clothing tips for each of the four business casual environments will illustrate how you can determine which options will work best for you.

Internal Environment

The internal environment is potentially the most casual of the four environments. Since there is generally no outside contact, the most casual options will apply.

- **Leggings:** As mentioned earlier, leggings can be risky, however, if they are worn with a long sweater that easily covers the thighs, they can be an option.

- **Shorts:** For warmer weather, walking shorts are comfortable options. The length should never be more than a few inches above the knee.

- **Sweatshirts and T-shirts:** These clothing items may be okay, but short-sleeved knits and shirts may be a better option.

- **Jeans:** And what about jeans? The good news is that they will work in some casual environments. Neat, clean jeans that are not bleached or torn, complimented by a shirt, blouse, or sweater, may be acceptable in many situations.

- **Shoes:** Shoes must always be in good condition— sneakers are no exception. Good alternatives to sneakers include: topsiders, loafers, leather shoes, and some canvas-style shoes. Boots work well with jeans, skirts, and slacks.

External Environment

In an external environment your daily activities and interactions with the public may vary. If you know you're going to have direct contact and be dealing face-to-face with someone (including customers), you should be aware of the impression you're going to make.

- **Jeans:** Jeans may be acceptable in some situations. Colored jeans will look dressier than blue jeans.

- **Blouse or Shirt:** A blouse or shirt in place of a T-shirt or sweatshirt will give you an upscale business casual look.

- **Jacket:** A jacket will also add to a coordinated casual look by communicating a sense of completion and polish. Keeping one nearby may be a good idea for those occasions when you wish to present yourself with more authority.

- **Shorts:** As in the internal environment, walking shorts are comfortable options for warmer weather. The length should never be more than a few inches above the knee.

- **Shoes:** Again, shoes must always be in good condition—sneakers are no exception. Good alternatives include: topsiders, loafers, and leather shoes. Boots work well with jeans, skirts, and slacks.

Traditional Environment

The traditional environment remains a little less flexible than the others. Business casual dress is basically a more casual version of the formal business look. Jeans, T-shirts, sweatshirts, shorts and sneakers are generally too casual and would not be considered appropriate in this environment. Pantsuits, jackets, shirts, and sweaters that are not as structured as typical business clothing may be worn. Such clothing is still less formal than the traditional corporate look.

- **Pantsuits and Skirts:** Pants have not always been an acceptable fashion for women in the workplace, but the recent return of the pantsuit provides a perfect choice for women wearing casual attire. Skirts also work well here.

- **Jacket:** Adding a jacket will upgrade your professional appearance. Again, it's always a good idea to keep a jacket close at hand.

- **Accessories:** Accessories will also enhance your basic look. Men can add a fun or interesting tie and women can add a scarf, earrings, or necklace.

- **Shoes:** Select shoes that coordinate well with your clothing. This may include the same styles you wear on any business day. Shoes that are clean, shined and in good condition are a must.

Your choices within the traditional environment can be somewhat limited but, nevertheless, represent a departure from the customary corporate look.

Social Environment

Social environments include a variety of situations. The company picnic and holiday party, for instance, are significant social events. They provide unique opportunities to get to know the people with whom you work. Even though these occasions take place during off-hours, it's still a business-related event. Choose your clothing carefully. Here are some tips that will help.

- If you're in charge of planning such an event, provide guidelines in your memo or invitation for what is appropriate attire: sport coat, no tie; or slacks but no jeans.

- If you're attending such an event, call the person hosting the event and ask what "casual attire" means.

- During warm weather, comfortable shorts (no more than three inches above the knee) and a shirt is your safest bet. Jeans, T-shirts, or sweatshirts are also practical. Muscle shirts, crop tops, and bathing suit tops are inappropriate.

- If you attend a convention, seminar or conduct business off-site, remember that these, too, are social environments. Always represent yourself and your company in the most positive way. *It's always better to be slightly over-dressed than under-dressed.* Tasteful, simple apparel is your safest choice.

Points to Remember

1. First, and most important, know your company's dress code or guidelines regarding casual dress. If your company has no formal or stated policy, ask *when* it is acceptable to wear casual clothes, and *what* is acceptable to wear. Make sure you know just *how* casual you can be in your particular workplace environment.

2. Choose a flattering style that *fits well*—nothing too big, too small, or too revealing.

3. Wear colors and patterns that coordinate—no crazy clashes just because you're casual. If you want more information on color, refer to the color section in Chapter Four.

4. When it comes to dressing casually you'll look—and be—successful by remembering this: it's casual *dress,* not casual *attitude.* Never forget that business is still business, even on casual dress day. Maintain your usual high standards of behavior and professionalism and you can't go wrong—whether you're in your power suit at the annual meeting or shorts and a T-shirt at the company picnic.

5. Look to managers and corporate officers for ideas on what to wear if you're in doubt.

Questions and Answers:

Casually Correct Dressing

1. The fit of your casual clothing is as important as the style and quality.

    TRUE.
    You can have the most stylish, expensive sweater or slacks, but if it pulls, puckers or hangs it will look cheap, and so will you. The way a garment fits is the most important aspect of looking good—whether you're casual, traditional, or somewhere in between.

2. The shoes you wear on casual dress day need not be in top condition.

    FALSE
    Shoes will be noticed. Wearing shoes and clothes in good condition is a *must*, on casual dress day and every day.

3. If you have clients coming to your facility for meetings on a casual dress day, notify them in advance, so they can choose whether or not to dress casually as well.

    TRUE.
    It is simple courtesy to let visitors know that they will be coming into a casual dress environment so they can choose, if they wish, to "dress down." They may choose to dress up anyway, even if their own company observes casual dress day, because they want to look businesslike for you. If you know your traditionally dressed client or customer will be visiting your office on casual dress day, dress traditionally yourself.

4. If your company has a casual dress policy, you must dress casually on casual-dress day.

   FALSE.
   Casual dress days are an option and a "perk," but are not mandatory. If you feel better or simply don't have casual clothing for work, it's quite acceptable to dress in your standard business attire.

5. It is not necessary to wear socks on casual dress day.

   FALSE
   To be clean and well-groomed, you should always wear socks under slacks or with shorts. Bare feet just aren't sanitary in an office setting, no matter which workplace environment.

6. On casual dress days, it is perfectly acceptable to save time by not washing your hair or taking a shower.

   FALSE.
   You and your hair must always be clean and fresh. If you normally can go a day without washing your hair, fine, but don't forget to comb and style it.

7. Men need not shave on casual dress days.

   FALSE.
   Remember, casual dress day is not sloppy day. Men must look clean and well-groomed, even on casual dress day. An unshaven look is never acceptable in an office environment.

8. Sunglasses and hats, visors, or caps are all casually correct business attire.

   FALSE.
   Sunglasses and headwear are *outdoor* gear, and thus should never be worn to work, except at an outdoor picnic, baseball game, or other outdoor event.

Details That
Make a Difference

Choosing and wearing the appropriate clothing isn't all there is to looking successful. Don't forget the finishing touches. Your general grooming, the appearance of your hair and nails, the accessories you wear, the condition of your clothing and even the eyeglasses you wear are part of your total look of success.

Exercise: Finishing Touches

Mark each question true or false, read through the chapter, then check your answers at the end.

1. Wear large rings, neck chains and earrings to show you are "fashion forward."   True/False

2. A great way to camouflage a bald spot is to grow your hair long on one side and comb it over the area where hair is thinning.   True/False

3. Glasses can make you appear more knowledgeable and intellectual.   True/False

4. Don't spend a lot of money on a pen. It's a disposable item and too easy to lose to justify a big investment. True/False

Grooming

Hair

If you're still wearing the same hairstyle you wore five years ago, it's time for a change. Often, people keep the same hairstyle for years because it reminds them of their youth or they associate that particular style with being in fashion. But in fashion when? Your cut and style should fit the business or industry with which you're involved and the style should involve very little maintenance during the day.

For men, hair should be no longer than the nape of the neck in back. For women, hair length is more flattering and professional when it's above the shoulders.

Alan, a successful business owner, offered to read my manuscript in its early stages. Because he has been so successful, I think we both assumed that he wouldn't learn anything new, but figured that the information would reinforce what he already knew. We were wrong. Not only did he pick up several ideas he planned on using with clients, but he made the decision to change his hairstyle. He had thinning hair and did what many men do—part it on the side in an attempt to cover the balding area. This chapter did it. He was motivated to change his hairstyle and the responses have been positive and subtle. Some people notice that he looks different, but they can't figure out what has changed.

If it's time for you to change your hairstyle, find a good stylist. A stylist does more than just cut hair. He or she will consult with you about what you like and dislike, and will consider your face shape, type and amount of hair and the type of work you do before recommending a particular style. Many stylists offer a free consultation during which they will ask questions such as: how much time are you willing to spend grooming your hair? What work do you do? What's your lifestyle and personality? What types of clothing do you wear most often? Your answers to these questions will help the stylist develop the right cut and hairstyle for you.

Some tips to help you decide on a hairstyle include:

- Avoid drastic changes.

- Use quality products to maintain healthy hair.

- Choose an easy-to-maintain style.

- Consider coloring your hair, which will bring out its highlights and may make you appear years younger.

Facial Hair

And what about facial hair? Some men grow a beard each winter and shave each summer. Most men with facial hair have had their beards or mustaches for many years. When I present a workshop, I always ask the men in the room with facial hair how long they've had it. And it never fails; I rarely hear, "Oh, I grew it last week." Instead, I hear five years, ten years, or more. Imagine, for some of these men, other people have never known them clean shaven! That's not bad, but any time we resist change, we might want to look at our reasons for doing so.

I always challenge these men to consider shaving just to see what lies beneath the hair on their faces. Many resist, but quite a few have accepted my challenge. I didn't realize how significant the change could be until I ran into a client, Greg, one day. After talking to him for several minutes, I finally said, "Greg, there's something different about you. Are you happier or something? You seem to be smiling more."

Greg replied, "No, I shaved my mustache." I hadn't actually noticed that about him, but I did notice a difference. I had never been able to see his mouth before, or his expression. When a mustache or beard obscures a man's facial muscles, others often have a hard time "reading" him. Some people actually interpret facial hair as rebellious or indicative of a need to hide something.

Facial hair is not always bad, however. In fact, for many men it enhances their looks or features. Facial hair can make a youthful, baby faced man look more mature. Someone losing hair on his head may balance his look by having hair on his face. The *safest* look in business is clean shaven, leaving nothing to be misunderstood. However, many industries have become relaxed enough so that a mustache poses no problem. Use a little more caution with beards. Judge whether or not a beard is appropriate based on your particular industry as well as your own preferences.

Fragrance

Use of cologne or perfume is acceptable but only if used lightly. Scent used too liberally can trigger sneezing, headaches and in general become overpowering for those around you.

Hands and Nails

Everyone notices hands and nails. If you make presentations or speeches, conduct meetings or seminars, or just shuffle papers during the day, your hands *will* be seen. Dry, chapped hands, ragged or bitten nails, hang nails and unclean fingernails will be noticed. Clean, well-manicured hands show you pay attention to detail.

Make sure your nails aren't too long. Many women enjoy acrylic nails and all of the jewelry art available for nails today. However, in business, extremely long nails are not a good idea. Because brighter colors are more visible, wearing bright colors draws attention to your nails. Bright colors, especially reds, are acceptable in some environments, but not conservative ones.

Avoid shocking fluorescent colors and dark browns, purples or black. One of the least expensive luxuries around is a professional manicure—treat yourself to one.

Grooming Checklist

Before you head out the door each morning, run through this checklist to make sure you've taken care of those final touches.

- Clothing clean and free of spots and stains?
- Garments well pressed?
- Clothing fits properly?
- Darker colors worn to convey authority?
- Socks lighter than or same color as shoes?
- Shoes darker or same color density as hem of skirt or slacks?
- Shoes and briefcase polished and in good condition?
- Hair neat, clean, well-styled, combed?
- Breath fresh?
- Hands well-groomed?

Last, before going out the door, check yourself from all angles in a full-length mirror to be sure that everything is in place, no slips showing, no buttons missing, no run in nylons, shirt not tucked in, etc.

Accessories

Choosing appropriate accessories can coordinate your overall look or change the look of the outfit you've selected to wear.

Jewelry

If the area that is pierced is unique, such as the eyebrow, nose, lip, tongue, etc., or you have many piercings, you separate yourself from the mainstream. This isn't always bad, but if your goal is to fit in and be recognized for your ideas and contributions, not your "look," it doesn't help you. Earrings for men should also be avoided. It simply isn't as common or acceptable for businessmen to wear earrings as it is for businesswomen. Earrings on men is a fashion or personal statement that may set you apart in your business. Much like ponytails on men, it just doesn't fit with a suit and professional look. If it's very important to you and symbolic of who you are, just realize you risk being perceived negatively by certain people who oppose the unique look you've chosen because of those symbols. The choice is yours. You're always *safest* when you fit into the norm.

The general rule about jewelry: Less is more. Avoid chunky jewelry—wear no more than one ring on any one finger, and no more than one ring on each hand. Buy good quality watches and jewelry; gold or better quality imitations are just fine. Tie tacks and clips are outdated and shouldn't be worn.

Belts, Wallets and Briefcases

In each case, buy good quality leather items. Avoid large belt buckles; a good rule of thumb is to choose the belt color to match your shoes. A slim wallet will fit more easily into your jacket pocket, without bulging. Your briefcase is a part of your total look and will be noticed if it is in poor condition. Keep it clean and polished. Buy a new one when it begins to look worn or frayed.

Pens

Buy and use a pen that is neither cheap nor overly expensive. A chewed up, 29 cent pen isn't going to contribute well to your overall professional image. While you don't need to spend a fortune, do purchase an attractive, good quality pen that is nice enough so you'll be sure not to lose it.

Eye wear

When was the last time you changed eye glasses? If it has been more than a couple of years, think about shopping for new frames. Eye wear should be current and flattering to the shape of your face. Avoid buying tinted glasses. Tints create odd skin coloration around the eyes and may block eye contact with others. Also, avoid frames that are distracting. Make sure your eyes are visible.

Before selecting new eye wear, think about the look you want to achieve. If you're young and wish to appear older or more knowledgeable, glasses can do the trick. The general perception is that glasses can serve to make you appear more mature, knowledgeable or intellectual. Frames are available today in fashionable styles and colors. Some people choose to buy several pairs and use them as an accessory to change their look.

If glasses are not something you enjoy or choose to wear, consider contact lenses. Contacts can be a great alternative to glasses, giving you the corrective lens you need without the bother of getting accustomed to frames.

Cosmetic Dentistry

A good smile is an important business tool. Fresh, clean teeth are a must. Proper hygiene, including flossing, checking your teeth often after eating and regular brushing are the minimum you need to do to take care of that smile. Visit your dentist for regular preventive maintenance check-ups and don't put off dental work suggested by your dentist.

Your smile is important in almost any situation, and if you're embarrassed by it, you won't use it. People have experienced personality changes as a result of cosmetic dentistry. If you are uncomfortable with your teeth, consider a visit to your dentist. Many adults have had their teeth bleached, or worn braces, retainers, and had a variety of other common procedures that affect how they look, smile and feel about themselves. As a result, they find themselves feeling more confident and pleased with their appearance.

Cosmetic dentistry works miracles! Teeth that are naturally yellow, crooked, chipped or cracked can be changed or repaired. Bleaching, bonding or applying laminate veneers are procedures often done to front teeth to correct the most visible tooth problems. Cosmetic dentistry can also involve straightening teeth that aren't aligned properly, filling in cracks or chips in damaged teeth or bleaching teeth that are discolored. Teeth that gap or overlap can also be corrected by your orthodontist. A confident smile is the goal. Another important reason for proper dental care is your breath. You can look great but if you have bad breath it will destroy your overall image. Good oral hygiene is the most important step to fresh breath. And do keep mints or breath fresheners around for those moments when you experience a bad taste in your mouth or can't get rid of the garlic from your lunch.

Clothing Maintenance

Now that you have some good quality clothes and accessories, maintain them. Dry clean your suits, ties, jackets and coats as needed, but not too often because the process is hard on the fabric. If you can afford it, use a professional laundering service to maintain your shirts; have them laundered and starched. Get rid of shirts that are frayed or yellowed. Use a fabric protector on ties to protect them from food spills and make them easier to clean.

Dry clean and launder regularly so you're never tempted to wear a soiled garment just because it's still hanging in your closet, ready to be chosen one morning when you're dressing in a hurry.

Keep suits and sport coats on their original hangers if possible. Other alternatives are wood, tubular or plastic-molded hangers. Curved hangers are bent because they help hold the shape of your jackets and prevent wrinkling or bulging in shoulders.

Store your shoes in shoe boxes to keep them clean and free of dust. These boxes can either be the original cardboard ones the shoes came in or plastic boxes sold in department and closet accessory stores. Cedar shoe trees are advantages for two reasons: they maintain the correct shape of your shoes during storage and they absorb moisture, which will extend the life of your shoes. Keep your shoes well-polished at all times. When buying shoes, purchase leather for better wear and fit.

In addition to clothing maintenance, don't forget *personal* maintenance. Bathe daily, use deodorant, brush your teeth, shave, wash, comb and style your hair. Do these daily maintenance steps without fail.

Points to Remember

1. Good grooming means an updated hairstyle, neatly trimmed mustache and beard and attention to personal cleanliness.

2. Accessories show your attention to detail in the quality and condition of jewelry, ties, belts, wallet, pen, briefcase, shoes and socks.

3. Eye wear can enhance your face, while making you look mature and knowledgeable. Keep it updated.

4. People notice hands. Well-manicured hands are a must.

5. Maintain your best professional tool—your smile! Pay attention to daily and preventive care. If you

hide your teeth, consult your dentist to make appropriate changes.

6. Good quality clothing must be maintained: dry
    clean, launder and use fabric protector on clothing.
    Polish your shoes.

7. Always make sure your clothing is clean and well-
    pressed, lint free and in good condition.

Questions and Answers:

Finishing Touches

At the beginning of this chapter, you answered four questions.
Now that you've read through the chapter, can you identify the
details that can make or break your look?

1. Wear large rings, neck chains and earrings to show
    you are "fashion forward."

    FALSE.
    The general rule about jewelry is: Less is more. Avoid
    chunky jewelry; wear no more than one ring on any
    one finger, and no more than one ring on each hand.
    Earrings for men should also be avoided in a busi-
    ness setting.

2. A great way to camouflage a bald spot is to grow
    your hair long on one side and comb it over the area
    where hair is thinning.

FALSE.

Don't try to pretend you're not losing your hair by stretching the last few strands across your head. Let your hair follow it's natural hairline. If you are uncomfortable with your hair loss, consider a hair transplant or a good quality hairpiece.

3. Glasses can make you appear more knowledgeable and intellectual.

    TRUE.

    Glasses in an up-to-date style that are flattering to your face can add a distinguished look. Glasses also make a younger person look older and wiser. Your eyes should always be visible behind your lenses. Save tinted lenses and wild, contemporary frames for the weekend.

4. Don't spend a lot of money on a pen. It's a disposable item and too easy to lose to justify a big investment.

    FALSE.

    Little things *do* make a difference. When you use a 29¢ pen (chewed on the end and missing its cap), you simply *don't* project a professional image. Every detail of your look should be consistent with the image you want to project—even something as small and seemingly insignificant as a pen. While you don't need to spend a fortune, do purchase an attractive, good quality pen that is nice enough that you'll be sure not to lose it.

Social Graces in Business Places

Etiquette is crucial to your professional success. Appropriate behavior and manners are just as important in the office as they are at a business lunch, formal black tie affair or social function related to business. *Understanding etiquette simply means knowing what to do, and how and when to do it.*

I've worked with companies that would never hire employees for an important position without first taking them out for dinner. Why? Because they want to see how the potential candidates handle themselves in a different, more relaxed atmosphere. Do they drink, smoke, tell offensive jokes? Do they know which fork to use? Since so many business transactions take place socially or over a meal, all of these things weigh heavily in a decision to hire.

Making others feel comfortable quickly is very helpful in any situation—initial meetings, business settings and social functions. When you handle all interactions smoothly, you convey a clear sense of competence and reliability. Knowing when and how to tip, pass the potatoes, or make small talk with someone you met five seconds ago will convey to anyone around you that you're worth getting to know!

View etiquette as a powerful tool to enhance your image. Look at it as an absolute, must-learn skill without which you simply can't move ahead. Etiquette finishes off an image that tells others you're savvy and in control.

Bill was well liked by everyone and had a successful sales future. He was welcomed by his clients but had a problem with his professional conduct. As you read the following story, see if you can find some of the reasons why Bill needs to brush up on his etiquette.

Bill had invited an important client and his wife to dinner. He scheduled it for 7:30 p.m. and selected an Italian restaurant. When Bill arrived, it was 7:45 and he realized he had forgotten to make reservations. The only available table was in the smoking section so, without asking his client, Bill accepted it. He didn't realize until later that his client's wife was allergic to smoke. When he did find out, he didn't offer to switch tables—he already knew another one wouldn't be available.

Bill forgot to tell his client that this was a casual restaurant, so while he had gone to his hotel to change into something more comfortable, his client went home to get dressed up. Bill ordered wine for the table, but found out his client doesn't drink and ended up drinking most of it himself. All seemed to be going well, but when the check came, it was quite a bit higher than Bill was expecting and he voiced his concern about his expense account...I think you get the picture.

It's true that some people, like Bill, are unskilled, yet successful in spite of themselves. But why do anything that might cause others to question your competency?

Bill should have given his client a few choices of restaurants and once a reservation was confirmed, let his client know the time, place and appropriate attire. What if his client didn't like Italian food or was allergic to tomatoes or cheese? Always ask whether the person you are with prefers smoking or non-smoking. When it comes to drinking alcohol, it's a good idea to observe what the other people are doing. It's perfectly fine not to drink. If you do drink, be sure not to drink too much. Know your capacity. Offer to be the designated driver if you feel you need a reason not to drink. Always arrange payment in advance, so it's not awkward when the bill is presented. Never make comments about the amount, whether you are the guest or host!

General Etiquette

Circle T or F after reading each statement below. Then read the chapter and check the answers at the end to see how much you've learned.

1. Good manners can be cost-effective.   True/False

2. When you're on the phone, your voice will come across more effectively and pleasantly if you smile.
   True/False

3. It's poor business practice not to return calls.
   True/False

4. Profanity can add impact if used sparingly.
   True/False

5. You should always plan to arrive at business events "fashionably late" which means about 5 to 10 minutes late.   True/False

6. A thank-you note can be handwritten.   True/False

7. When a man and woman approach a door, the person who reaches it first should open it.   True/False

8. Use your first and last name when calling someone.
   True/False

An associate of mine who coaches people on image development once worked with a prominent surgeon. This surgeon, about to attend an important conference, felt ill-at-ease and self conscious about his ability to handle himself effectively with his colleagues. Referring to himself as awkward, he desperately wanted to gain control over his behavior and reputation. Ironically, here was a man capable of performing complex surgery, yet concerned with his image and ability to act with ease in social situations. He knew a clearer understanding of etiquette was to his advantage and was willing to seek help. With coaching, he made small but significant changes that greatly improved his social skills.

Sometimes the more skilled we are in our technical or product expertise, the more we rely on that knowledge rather than our ability to interact with others. There are people with much academic or technical knowledge who don't have a clue when it comes to communication and social interaction. Sometimes people hide behind their degrees, awards and certificates of achievement, never fully feeling capable in any other arena. *The key is balance.*

All Interactions Are Important

Think of each interaction you have on the job, including social functions, as an important opportunity to build relationships. Whether you're greeting the office receptionist in the morning, returning a phone message to a not-so-key potential client or presenting a top priority report to the board of directors, any exchange could be the most important one you're going to have today.

Why this emphasis on every little interaction? First, any business situation represents an opportunity of some kind. And second, even small exchanges help you practice polishing your skills. Also, each interaction builds a larger sense of your presence within your office environment. Your reputation for handling situations competently and discreetly will go before you, so that you become known very quickly, and on all levels, as a person of quality, reliability and professionalism.

General Demeanor: Know the Unwritten Rules

I'm no longer surprised at the absence of etiquette in the world of business. For some reason, the company holiday party, picnic or other social event often becomes an opportunity for some employees to let their hair down—dancing on tables, falling in love for one night, drinking too much, etc. Let me assure you, this kind of behavior has sabotaged careers. Although business social events provide opportunities to build bonds and foster relationships, they're still *business*. You do want to be taken seriously. So don't be uptight, but always be in control!

Every office, every business, every industry has its own unwritten code of behavior and rules. You can learn your workplace etiquette simply by watching those around you. You might be fortunate enough to have a mentor who is willing to teach you the rules, including that silent code. But if you don't have such a person or network in your life, observe people you admire or hold positions you strive to obtain. Watch for the quiet clues: how they look, act and present themselves. Your goal is to look and act like someone who is already where you want to be.

Here are some ideas that will help you develop a polished, professional manner in all interactions you have during the course of a day.

- **Respect time:** Be on time. Respect other people's schedules. Meet all deadlines: on time, on budget.

- **Be a problem solver:** Put in the extra time needed to do the job right. Be creative, treat problems as challenges just waiting for the right solution.

- **Be discreet:** Discretion is necessary at all times. Don't get involved in personal relationships on-the-job *or* at social functions related to the job that can interfere with job performance. Show respect for all people, at all levels, during all transactions, on or off the job.

- **Stay on task:** If it doesn't have to do with the company goals or with the goals you need to accomplish, ignore it! That means avoiding gossip, relationships, office politics and other distractions to remain clearly focused on specific work tasks you're responsible for completing.

- **Be positive at all times:** Offices are full of gripes, complaints, problems and general morale issues. All companies function with ups and downs; don't criticize people or the company out loud. Acknowledge the reality of the situation and get on with it! Operate by this simple rule of thumb: If it's negative, ignore it! And, you can go one step further: Be a leader and encourage those around you to focus on the positive.

- **Think before you speak:** Play the devil's advocate with yourself and think through what you want people to know and what you want them to do. Anticipate the effect of what you're saying or proposing and of course, never act or speak when you're angry. If you have an issue with someone or something in the office, be sure to talk to the appropriate person; be prepared and calm.

In addition to the above points, professional behavior also involves keeping your word. *Say what you mean and mean what you say.* People can only count on you when you're reliable. Think about all of the times we say things to people we might not really mean or we tell others what we think they want to hear. How often do you say, "I'll call you tomorrow" and never do that, or say something like, "Let's get together soon" and allow months to go by before you make an effort to call. Though those little comments are rarely taken seriously, you don't want to lose your reputation for sincerity.

How often do we tell people what they want to hear? How often are we truly accountable for what we say? When was the last time you said you'd be there at 2 o'clock and showed up at 2:10? Or that you'd return a call and didn't? It's the little comments that make or break trust. Other people need to believe that what you say is what you will do. *Nothing is more important than your word.*

Other general demeanor tips to remember include the following:

- Memorize people's names and use them. Repeat a name after hearing it and use it often when speaking to the person.

- Be on time. Always plan to arrive five to ten minutes *early* so you won't hold things up and will be ready to start on time.

- Organize yourself, your desk, office, even your car. Make sure all aspects of you are presented in a clean, neat and orderly way.

- Speak articulately and grammatically using clear concepts and good diction.

- Know how the managers and executives in your company dress, how they behave, how they present themselves—and do the same.

Introductions

If you're confused about the proper way to introduce or be introduced, here are some simple rules to remember and practice. The general rule of thumb in business situations is: the person who is more honored, or who has the higher rank is named first, while the other person(s) is presented to him or her. For example, "Mr. President, I'd like to introduce you to John Doe."

Here are some examples of appropriate and inappropriate responses used during introductions:

Say...	Not...
• It's nice to meet you.	• It's nice to know you. (You don't.)
• How do you do?	• Charmed. (Are you?)
• I've heard many good things about you	• I've heard about you. (Leaves the person wondering what you heard.)

Who's responsible for doing the introductions? Generally, the host or hostess is responsible for introductions. In a business setting, that means the person in whose office the meeting takes place, the person who called the meeting, or the most senior member of the group, if he or she had some responsibility for calling the gathering together. If two people are equally responsible for calling a meeting, then they should determine in advance who is going to do the introductions.

It is also appropriate for whoever knows both parties to introduce those who don't know each other. Introductions should be done immediately. There's nothing more uncomfortable than standing around, without being introduced, while others are talking and laughing together. So rule number one: Introduce people who don't know each other immediately! And remember that you can always introduce yourself.

What about situations in which the key person might not know all the names? This could happen, for example, if a focus group is assembled from a variety of professions to discuss a common purpose. There may be people attending who don't know each other and might not know you. It is appropriate, in this case, for you to introduce yourself, brief everyone on why you've brought them together, and then allow each person to introduce himself or herself. You'll want to structure these self-introductions, though, by saying something like, "I'd like each of you to introduce yourself, telling us your name, the company or organization you represent and what your primary interest is in attending this meeting." That way, each person can do some quick mental preparation before being asked to speak. You'll also minimize the time introductions take by structuring what you want each person to say.

When you're introduced to others, offer your hand immediately, and shake hands firmly. Make eye contact while shaking hands and smile warmly. Say something in your greeting that's general but gracious and noncommittal, such as, "I'm very pleased to meet you." Repeat the person's name in your greeting to help you remember it: "Hello, Chris. It's nice to meet you." If you're introduced to several people, shake hands with each just after the introduction—don't wait until all have been introduced. That way you can acknowledge and make contact with each in turn, rather than making a collective gesture of greeting.

Something magical happens when you take the time to connect with another person. After finalizing a program with a company, the man who hired me wanted to introduce me to the people with whom I'd be working. I met twelve people. We shook hands and exchanged greetings. Yet only one of these people had an impact on me. I left thinking about this person trying to figure out why he'd made me feel so welcome, appreciated and connected to him. I realized it was the sincerity of the handshake and the length of eye contact that had done it.

Try it. Look longer and put more sincerity in your handshake. So often in the course of the day, we simply go through the motions of greeting new people. For example, how often have you gone through the act of meeting someone without actually hearing their name? Slow down, concentrate and make an effort to really connect with people. These steps will make a difference.

In my seminars, I often ask each person to introduce himself or herself to someone else in the group. I allow two to three minutes for them to get acquainted, which helps people relax. Once back in their seats, I ask them to take out paper and pencil and write down three things: The first name of the person they just met, the last name and the color of his or her eyes. The response is often laughter mixed with sighs, moans and groans.

While about 40 percent remember the first name, very few remember both first and last name. And less than half can name the eye color correctly. Some even admit that their correct eye color answers were pure guesswork! So, the next time you meet someone, look him or her in the eye long enough to remember eye color. Repeat the name so you'll remember it. That little bit of effort can go a long way toward creating a lasting connection.

When introducing someone, give other information such as first and last name, company or organization the person is associated with or other history. This information will give others a basis for conversation and might help someone who can't quite place the person being introduced. Avoid using first names too soon after first meeting. If you're not at the same rank, use the other person's professional title (i.e., Judge, Doctor, Professor, Mr., Mrs., Ms.). It's always appropriate to tell others how you'd like to be addressed: "Please call me Sue. What do you wish to be called?"

And last, always rise when meeting someone: that shows respect and interest. The etiquette of introductions might vary in some special situations, but in general, the rules hold whether you're in a business, social/business, or other settings.

Just remember that introductions are an essential function that should be done immediately.

Written Correspondence

Memos are a primary form of written business correspondence, ranging in use from "Meet me for lunch at Tony's" to "Bring your full report to the investor's meeting and be prepared to present it." You find yourself presenting yourself on paper frequently, and to many people. How you look on paper has its first impression, too. If you make a mistake, it will be remembered for a long time.

Do you ever get memos with your own name misspelled? Or one with a typo? How about a memo with incorrect information or the wrong meeting time or place that has to be followed up with a memo correcting the first memo? Any one of these things has a tendency to be remembered. Two or more of these kinds of correspondence errors *really* stick to you.

New technologies have produced "netiquette," to be used in e-mail correspondence. Basically, the same rules apply when communicating electronically as when communicating with paper. Remember, many people may see a message intended for one person. Always keep this in mind when writing e-mail. It's easy to forget to proofread or spell check something on e-mail, but grammar, spelling and punctuation is as important in electronic communications as in any other communication.

All memos and other written correspondence should be prepared as you would a speech or other verbal presentation. Written messages or information can convey several different meanings, depending upon word choice, content, etc. The overall impression a written document makes depends on grammar, punctuation, spelling, accuracy of content and neatness of format.

To make a positive impression when you're conveying something in writing, follow these tips.

- If your signature is being used, read it personally. Don't depend on anyone else for final proofreading.

- If your signature is required, sign it yourself. Don't allow someone else to sign your name.

- Proofread all correspondence. Check for grammar, punctuation, spelling and correct name.

- Make sure all written documents are clearly and neatly formatted so they're easy to read and look professional.

- Print all written correspondence or other reports or documents on good quality paper using a high resolution printer.

- Check and double check content for accuracy. If the meeting is going to be in the "A" conference room at the Savannah Hotel at noon, double check all the details with the hotel before the memo goes out.

- If you have to send a memo out to correct a problem or mis-statement of some kind, don't blame anyone. Simply state the correction and apologize briefly for any inconvenience caused.

- Handwritten notes are acceptable, but they must be legible. They can be used to show personal time and sincerity, especially in thank-you notes.

I once worked with a man named Kim. When I was out of the office, I had my assistant draft a memo to Kim to get it out that day. When I returned to the office, I found to my horror that the memo was addressed to Ms. Kim Smith—and I had my secretary sign my name to the memo as well! I was very embarrassed and made an apology. I had met with Kim face-to-face so, of course, I knew he was a man. I learned never to let anything with my name go out unless I've read it. I now sign all of my own correspondence.

Another time I had a proposal go out without seeing it first. Only after it was too late, I noticed spelling and other errors...a hard way to learn an important lesson. I've learned never to assume anything and to be very specific with every detail when turning things over to my assistant. After all, the final responsibility lies with me, not anyone else.

When using fax as a means of written communication, follow a few basic guidelines:

- Call to notify the person you're faxing to expect a fax, including the number of pages.

- Always follow up faxing by mailing a hard copy if the document is important and should be retained in files for future reference.

- Don't fax thank-you notes or letters.

- Number each page and the total number of pages you are sending.

- Make sure your fax and phone numbers are on the cover page.

Telephone Calls and Voice-Mail Messages

In telephone and voice mail interactions, your voice says it all. Face-to-face, your gestures, eyes, posture, facial expressions, stance and body movements all influence what the listener hears and the meaning he or she ascribes to what you say. Phone and voice-mail exchanges eliminate these nonverbal cues, forcing the listener to focus solely on your words and tone. *Remember, how you say it and your tone of voice is more important than what you say.*

In voice mail exchanges, use the technology to your advantage. I've set up appointments, meetings and lunch dates through voice mail without ever directly talking to the people involved. If you're friendly and efficient, you can make a great impression by using voice-mail savvy! You can encourage people to make decisions with an urgent-sounding voice-mail message. I've left stern, firm and direct messages on voice mail, often in frustration after repeated calls have been left unanswered. How amazing it is that, with the right tone and message, we can get people to respond!

Here's an example that illustrates the importance of professional phone voices. I consulted with the ticket department of a national football team. The salespeople sold season tickets and had to deal with happy as well as unhappy fans. They wanted my help to improve their customer service and overall professionalism. I learned that each person answered the phone differently. Together we planned a uniform greeting and closing. They agreed that this would make a big difference in customer satisfaction. Their attitudes when answering the phone could change the customers' impressions of them.

How do you answer your calls? Does your greeting convey warmth and friendliness? Do you sound rushed or hassled? Think about the impression you want to make and plan a greeting accordingly.

In phone conversations, you're judged by the emotional quality in your voice. That emotional quality is affected by whether or not you're stressed, tired or impatient. If you're speaking fast or slow, loud or soft, or in a monotone without expression, you're giving some other, unintended messages as well.

Did you know that your mental and emotional state causes physiological changes in your body, changes that can affect your voice? For example, if you're stressed, the tension in your body constricts muscles, including those in your face and around your mouth and throat. Tighter muscles in these areas change the quality of your voice. Before getting on the phone, take a few deep breaths to relax. This will help the tonal quality of your voice, as well as the pace of your message. Clear your throat *before* you pick up the phone. Keep water nearby and drink plenty of it if you use your voice frequently. Record some telephone answering machine or voice mail messages and play them back. Re-record until you're satisfied with how you sound.

Many people change their messages daily, stating the date, their whereabouts, and their availability. When you find the right words, practice how you say them. And watch out for the deadly monotone that creeps into many of our recorded messages!

Don't say you'll return a call if you're not going to. We are all beginning to use voice mail and most of us leave a standard message: can't take your call right now, leave a message and I'll get back to you as soon as I can." Yet most of us lie! Many never intend to return calls at all, yet leave a message that says we will. If you know you will not return calls, do not say that you will! If you receive so many calls that you cannot possibly return them all, then either have someone else return them for you or state on your message that you cannot return all calls. Suggest they send you something in writing, but do not make promises you will not keep. Start paying attention to all the excuses people give you for failing to return a phone call. "I've been so busy." "We've been bogged down." "The work load is incredible." "I've been out all week." What all of this really says is, "I'm too busy to call you—you're not that important."

If the president of a company or an important client left you a message, you *would* find the time to call him or her back. The fact is, we're all guilty of making judgments and assumptions about the intentions of others. Although it might be a perfectly natural reaction to be put off by calls from those you don't know, especially when they might be trying to sell you something, you never know what opportunity that call might present.

I've dealt with company presidents who I would never have expected to return my calls; they did. And I've worked with other people who *never* returned my calls, even after we'd met and they'd promised a return call. Returning calls promptly says something about you and your professionalism. What kind of reputation do you want to have?

The etiquette of telephone and voice-mail messages is simple.

- Answer as many calls as you can in person.

- Always answer your phone by the third ring. If you can't answer your phone that quickly, have someone else do it or switch on your voice mail.

- If you can't return a call, leave a message that states you cannot return all calls. Suggest that the caller mail his or her request or information to you.

- Leave a warm and welcoming message that conveys as closely as possible when you'll be able to return calls.

- Always identify yourself by your first and last name when calling someone and, in most cases, your company name as well. Except for close business associates with whom you talk frequently, do not assume the person you're calling will know who you are without identification.

- Return calls promptly, within one business day.

- Return *all* calls; even unknown callers might represent potential opportunities.

- If you can't return your calls personally, have someone else get back to the callers on your behalf.

- Don't wait until after-business hours to return calls. Many people do this solely because they can leave voice mail messages, effectively shortening the total time it takes to return calls. All you gain is time. You lose your edge in being able to control your image, message and sense that you're ready to take on whatever the challenge is and find solutions—now.

- Don't put anyone on hold for more than 20 seconds without checking back and giving the caller the option to continue holding, leave a message or call back.

- As much as possible, do not pass messages to others to handle. Doing so sends a message to the callers that they are not important enough for you to personally respond. Return your own calls so you're in a key position both to know what's going on and to offer your skill or expertise to the situation at hand.

- Don't coach secretaries or receptionists to screen calls in a way that is obvious to the caller. Saying "I'll see if he's available. May I tell him who's calling?" is a polite way to learn the caller's identity, and allow you to determine whether you want to take the call at that moment. But again, take as many calls as you can. Messages just pile up for later, and you sacrifice that sense of immediacy, readiness and availability that can be very important in relations with clients, customers and co-workers.

- Keep messages you leave on voice mail short and to the point. State your name and number clearly.

- Remember to speak slowly when leaving a telephone number or address. Someone on the other end will need to write it down.

- Always repeat your name and telephone number at the end of your message

A seminar participant, Leslie, once shared a great story about not returning phone calls. Once when she needed some legal advice, Leslie called and left a message with an attorney in another town who had been highly recommended to her. He didn't call her back, so after a week or so she hired another attorney. *Two months later,* Leslie received a collect call from the first attorney. Obviously, Leslie had no business to give him and, put out by the collect call, told him so.

At a meeting some six months later, Leslie was introduced to this same attorney. He said, "Your name is so familiar—do I know you?" Leslie replied, "Well, I called you about six months ago. It took you two months to return the call and then you called collect—but no, we've never met!" Embarrassed, the attorney replied, "Gee, I'm sorry. I didn't realize you were a client of mine." "I'm not," Leslie answered, "But I *could* have been had you returned my call!"

Early in my business career, I approached the president of a major retail chain as a potential client. Not only did I get through to him personally, but he gave me an appointment for the next day. Although he didn't know me, and was a busy man, he was willing to reach out rather than use his secretaries to fend off callers. His business is thriving. His accessibility to a perfect stranger reflects his openness to the people who work for him as well. What an impression he has made on me and how rare to find that kind of accessibility in a busy chief executive! The moral: Failing to return or accept calls limits you. You convey a nonverbal message to those you avoid: "I'm not interested in you, I'm too busy." *Being accessible will improve your image and potential for success.*

Don't ever assume anything! I receive many calls soliciting my business and try to practice what I preach by returning every call I receive. On one occasion, I had recently been featured on the news and was receiving many calls. One was from a printer and the message was simply to call Rhoda at XYZ Printers. I called back to see what she wanted, but she was unavailable. I assumed she wanted to try to solicit my business for printing and said "Tell her Sue Morem called. I am returning her call and you can tell her I'm not interested in any printing. I am very happy with the printer I am using." Well, Rhoda called me back and let me know that she was not trying to sell me printing or get my business. She actually had a business opportunity for me—she was looking for a speaker for an annual meeting. I was embarrassed and apologized, but knew I had blown it. Not a great first impression. Do you think I got the job? No, I did not, and I didn't expect to. But I did learn a valuable lesson. Don't jump to conclusions, and always leave a bit of information as to what you're calling about when you leave a message to help others avoid the same kind of mistake I made.

When you make outgoing calls, basic rules of etiquette are important as well. Recall the habits and mannerisms that irritate you when you take calls from others and avoid doing those things yourself. Practice your opening words so you always sound confident and friendly in those crucial first few seconds. Remember, first impressions happen whether the contact is made in person or by phone. Your opening words, your tone, pitch and the warmth of your voice in general will make a lasting impression.

If you can't get people to return *your* calls, consider that they might be sending you a message saying they are not interested or simply have no time to call. If you have left several messages, get creative. Try talking to the receptionist or secretary to find out the best time to reach someone. Vary the times of your calls to increase your chance of connecting. Call before 9:00 a.m. or after 5:00 p.m. and you just may reach the person before or after the normal work day hours.

Here's a list of good telephone protocol. When these rules are violated, we often feel put off, even angry. Circle those rules that you personally *most* dislike to have violated. Then hold that thought—you'll remember to be sure not to do those things to others when phoning and leaving messages. Add a check mark to those you know you need to work on.

Telephone advice to consider:

- Good telephone etiquette requires that all phone calls be returned within one business day.

- Make sure you have a purpose for your call: a call interrupts someone.

- Get to the point, avoid lengthy small talk.

- Give oral feedback, don't let your listener hang in silence.

- Don't eat, smoke, or chew gum while on the phone; avoid other background distractions (rustling paper, radio, etc.).

- Don't use the speaker phone without the caller's permission.

- If you reach a wrong number, apologize.

- If a caller dials your number by mistake, graciously tell him or her that he or she reached a wrong number.

- Avoid calling anyone at home before 8 a.m. and after 10 p.m.

- Give full attention to the person on the telephone.

- If disconnected, the person who placed the call should reestablish the call.

- Answer the telephone by the third ring.

- Don't take calls when someone is in your office.

- If a call comes when you're in someone's office, and he or she needs to take the call, offer to step outside.

- Identify yourself when making a call.

- Smile while on the phone.

- Be aware of your tone of voice.

- Don't say you will return a call unless you know you will.

Office Etiquette

Who sits first? Who sits where at a meeting? Who should be the first to signal an end to a meeting or business interaction? These interactions can happen smoothly if you have a sense of general office etiquette. Reacting quickly conveys a tremendous sense of poise and presence likely to be noted by others.

First, a few words about general office etiquette. Some of the guidelines we've discussed earlier apply here, and are worth mentioning again.

1. Be on time and respect other people's time.

2. Treat all people with equal respect—treat them as you would like to be treated, and do so in all situations.

3. Be a positive problem solver in all circumstances. Handle problems, rudeness, anger, or complaints of others in a detached, unemotional, matter-of-fact way.

4. When someone enters your office, stand and extend your hand.

5. Never drop in to visit someone unexpectedly. Always call ahead.

When you enter someone else's office, knock, wait for him or her to offer you a seat or acknowledge you in some other way. If a handshake isn't offered, go ahead and offer your hand to break the ice. In meetings, allow others on a higher level to seat themselves first. Select a seat in which you will feel comfortable, but do it discreetly, quietly, and graciously—no clumsy jockeying for position.

Where you sit in a meeting does make a difference. The most powerful position is at the head of the table, facing the door. This allows the person in charge to see who is coming and going. There are varying opinions on where to sit. Some experts say the middle of the table is the most influential. Anytime you are across a table or desk from someone, because there is a barrier between you, it is less cordial and potentially more threatening than if you are on the same side of a table or a desk. If you are having difficulty working with someone, try switching positions and getting on the same side of things.

When you bring documents to the office of someone sitting behind a desk, ask permission to come around to where he or she is sitting so you both can see the documents better. Or suggest that the other person come around and join you in the chair alongside so you can review the document together. If *you're* the one behind the desk, greet your visitor, seat him or her in a setting with two chairs situated side-by-side, and then sit down in the other chair.

When more than one person enters your office, stand, greet them warmly, shake hands, and immediately indicate with a hand gesture where you would like each to sit. If they are carrying coats, let them know where to put them and then indicate which chairs you'd like them to take. Wait until your guests are seated before you sit down and wait to be seated until invited to do so when you're in someone else's office.

Gender And Diversity

Gender issues do not have to be difficult. If you operate by one simple rule, you'll probably never find yourself wondering how to handle potential gender issues. The rule: *treat men and women equally.*

In my newspaper column, I answered a man who was avoiding women altogether in the workplace because he was afraid of offending them. He wondered how women wanted to be treated. I responded saying that he should treat women like he would treat men—basically treating all people with respect. The women's response to my comments were positive; the men were outraged. Women said, "right on!" and men said, "Women are so sensitive that we have to walk on eggshells around them."

Although the battle of the sexes continues, treating all people with professional respect, regardless of gender, status, or any other difference is just common sense. I'm talking about the basics here, just a few simple courtesies that help establish boundaries and expectations. Among the greatest concerns for business are the issues of both workplace diversity and sexual harassment. Managers and staff are expected to treat everyone with professional courtesy and respect all the time.

Observing a few formal rules of professional conduct, such as arriving on time, making introductions smoothly, and sticking to business topics in conversation so everyone is comfortable eliminates misinterpretation and misunderstanding. Your business transactions aren't clouded with distracting questions such as, "What did that remark mean? Did I write down the wrong time? Is she ignoring me because I did something wrong? Are people of my race (or gender or ethnic background) not welcomed here?"

Treating everyone with respect is simple, easy to remember and easy to interpret in all circumstances. Remember to apply the same etiquette and fairness rules in social situations that overlap with work. Office parties, business lunches or out-of-town travel shouldn't create a question in your mind about how to behave: The same rules of day-to-day office and business etiquette apply. Many people have made major mistakes by stepping over that professional boundary outside the office. Don't make that same mistake. Social/work functions can tempt you into indiscreet behavior or remarks with co-workers. These acts and comments will visit you again, probably in an unfavorable way.

Don't go out of your way to run to the door first to open it or block an elevator entrance when you're in front just to let a woman out first, etc. Whoever is at the door first should open it. Whoever is at the front of the elevator should walk out first. If someone needs help getting a coat on, help him or her. While there's no need to jump up to pull out a chair, rising is a nice gesture—for both women and men.

Points to Remember

1. Consider business etiquette one of the most important skills you can develop to help you meet your career goals.

2. Shake hands firmly, warmly and often.

3. Be just as polite and resourceful in phone, fax, voice mail and written correspondence as you are during in-person interactions.

4. Approach men and women equally, including the handshake, office demeanor and respectful, competent business interactions.

Questions and Answers:

General Etiquette

How do your answers to the quiz you took at the beginning of the chapter compare with those below?

1. Good manners can be cost-effective.

    TRUE.
    Acting properly and treating people well makes good business sense. Good manners bring you a good reputation and allow little room for your actions to be misunderstood. Negative behavior can cost a promotion, a job, a customer/client and even result in decreased productivity and profit. Poor manners shows ignorance, lack of knowledge and awareness and may be interpreted as shallow or uncaring.

2. When you're on the phone, your voice will come across more effectively and pleasantly if you smile.

    TRUE.
    Simply smiling does put a smile in your voice! Since the person you are talking with can't see you, you need to work hard at injecting enthusiasm in your voice.

3. It's poor business practice not to return calls.

    TRUE.
    There's no excuse for failing to return calls. Though you might be busy or have an important title, not returning calls is always discourteous. When you are in the office, return all calls within one business day. When you're out of the office, let the person who's

taking your calls know when to tell callers they can expect you to call back. Or leave the appropriate message on your answering machine or voice mail. Don't say, "I'll get back to you as soon as possible" if you know you won't.

4. Profanity can add impact if used sparingly.

    FALSE.
    Swearing is never impressive. It actually diminishes your credibility and impact by making you look out of control. Remain cool and calm and avoid swearing or slang.

5. You should always plan to arrive at business events "fashionably late" which means about 5 to 10 minutes late.

    FALSE.
    There's no such thing as fashionably late. Late is late and is inconsiderate whether it's 5, 10 or 30 minutes. Always plan to arrive 5 to 10 minutes early so you won't hold things up and will be ready to start on time.

6. A thank-you note can be handwritten.

    TRUE.
    A handwritten thank-you note can be appropriate and more personal than a typewritten one. Make sure your handwriting is legible and that your thoughts are sincere. A thank-you note, handwritten or typed, should be written for all gifts and is appropriate for even small favors or gestures of kindness. Thanking someone for his or her time, appointments, etc., is an

important and gracious gesture. Handwritten envelopes generally are opened before typewritten or labeled ones.

7. When a man and woman approach a door, the person who reaches it first should open it.

TRUE.
Not only men can be polite and helpful. Opening a door is a matter of common, gender-free courtesy. Who's there first and whose hands are free override gender.

8. Use your first and last name when calling someone.

TRUE.
It is most professional to introduce yourself with a first and last name. Never assume the person knows you well enough, unless it's someone you deal with regularly, to forego association with your company, as well. The person you're calling probably receives many calls each day and may be unable to place every Chris and Kelly without direct identification.

Maintaining Professionalism in Any Situation

There really is a fine art involved in making conversation. The need for small talk and interesting conversation often occurs more in business social situations. Listening is also an important skill to learn.

Once again you might be asking yourself, "What has this got to do with professionalism? Do I really have to spend time learning how to chit-chat with people?" The answer, once again, is yes, absolutely! Conversation forms the foundation for business deals and relationships. Your conversational skills can help you:

- Appear capable and friendly.

- Create strong relationships with clients, customers or key people in your organization.

- Set the background for negotiating business or set the tone for important meetings.

- Identify potential clients or new business.

- Network, gather information or keep up-to-date on industry, business or client/customer trends.

- Establish yourself as a good listener and sound resource.

So you've been seated next to someone you've just been introduced to a few minutes ago. Where do you start?

In his book, How to Win Friends and Influence People, Dale Carnegie says you can make more friends in two months by becoming interested in other people than you can in two years by trying to get other people interested in you.

Here are some do's and don'ts in the art of conversation:

- **Educate yourself.** At a minimum, read newspaper headlines, watch the first five minutes of the television news or check the internet for headlines so you know the latest news. Take time to read as much as you can to have a current knowledge of a variety of topics. In conversation, show your interest in a wide area of subjects. In-depth discussion of a few topics is less ideal than general knowledge of many things. For one thing, you won't intimidate those you're conversing with by delving too deeply into topics they might be unfamiliar with. The art of good conversation leaves your listeners with their egos intact!

- **Learn to remain quiet and listen.** Often the art of really good conversation is not saying anything at all! Good listeners enjoy listening and sincerely believe that what the person is talking about is important. This skill translates to making the person feel interesting and important. Good listening habits also prevent you from interrupting, overpowering conversations, or generally coming off in a pompous or overbearing way.

I was at a convention when I struck up a conversation with Mary, the life of the party and event. Her stories had everyone around her listening, laughing and asking for more. As we sat by each other through dinner, I asked questions and she told me story after story. I enjoyed her and learned a great deal. When I got up to leave, she said, "Good-bye. It was great talking with you—I really enjoyed it!" The truth was I barely said a word but she thought I was the great conversationalist! Any time we ask questions, we show we're interested in others and what they have to say. Asking questions to get others to talk is the best way to become a great conversationalist.

- **Learn graceful ways to change the subject.** When silences loom, interest in particular topics wanes, or a slightly embarrassing comment needs to be covered, learn to control conversations by deftly changing to another subject.

  Asking a question can provide a good opportunity to change subjects: "Has anyone heard the weather forecast for this weekend?"

- **Develop skill in drawing others into a conversation.** Quiet people or newcomers might need a bit of help to enter the conversation successfully. Focusing your eyes on and including someone can accomplish this: "John, I heard you're an avid skier. How did you get started?"

- **Use techniques to make people feel comfortable.** Remember names and use them often, ask questions, listen carefully to responses, use your previous knowledge of the person's interests or history and the person's current responses to build on conversation.

"Weren't you going on a trip the last time I saw you?" "I heard you moved recently. Where? How did it go?"

- **Ask questions.** By asking questions you indicate that you're listening and interested in what others are saying. "How did you get into this line of work?" Or "How did you get involved in the Chamber?" are good conversation openers.

- **Avoid interrupting others.** Interruptions can take the form of correcting others, breaking eye contact by looking elsewhere, fidgeting, changing the subject or speaking off-topic. This indicates you weren't really listening to the exchange. Any of these actions leave others feeling slighted in some way. They might even be a bit angry with you without your even being aware of it. The only time interrupting may be appropriate is when someone is monopolizing the conversation or meeting.

- **Don't say too much about yourself.** While you don't want to be too secretive or private, don't monopolize the conversation either.

- **Be upbeat and positive.** Share the positive things others have done and concentrate on generally positive, upbeat topics. Don't try to solve world problems over a "happy" hour.

- **Stick with safe topics.** There's nothing worse than an animated conversation at a cocktail party about death, dying, cancer and crime. General topics, such as sports, weather, hobbies and work, keep you on firm ground.

- **Make good eye contact with others.** Look directly at people, engage them by linking eyes as well as hands through a handshake in greeting and parting. Then take time to listen. Show real interest in others. Ask questions, listen to responses so you can learn more about the other person and perhaps even discover some real common ground or shared interest that sparks a genuine connection. Then you have a foundation for developing firm relationships that form solid groundwork for on-the-job allies, networking, mentoring, and/or good customer or client relations.

- **Avoid gossip.** Refrain from talking about others in a negative way. Those who talk to you about others will also talk about you to others.

- **Learn to receive and give compliments.** A modest smile, an appreciative nod or even turning the compliment into an opportunity to acknowledge others will help you accept compliments without seeming either overbearing or passive. A simple thank you is always appropriate.

How Well Do You Listen?

Studies have shown that most of us listen poorly, missing much of what is communicated. How well do you listen?

Do you:

- Look at the person talking to you (maintain eye contact)?   Yes/No

- Avoid interrupting?   Yes/No

- Ask questions? Clarify?   Yes/No

- Become agitated with disagreements?   Yes/No

- Avoid distractions?   Yes/No

- Avoid completing other people's sentences?   Yes/No

- Avoid correcting other people's grammar or word choice?   Yes/No

- Give feedback/response?   Yes/No

- Keep background distractions to a minimum (reading mail, looking through papers, watching people walk by, etc.)?   Yes/No

- Wait to answer questions until the speaker is finished posing them?   Yes/No

- Show interest in the conversation through verbal feedback?   Yes/No

- Show interest through nonverbal feedback (nodding, facial expression)?   Yes/No

- Avoid changing subject abruptly?   Yes/No

If you have answered yes to many or all of these questions, congratulations! You're a great listener. If you've answered no, you might need to polish up your listening skills a bit. Which skills from this list do you need to work on?

avoid distractions	give feedback
lean forward	ask for clarification
avoid interrupting	take more notes
ask more questions	lean forward
make consistent eye contact	

What actions will you take to improve your listening skills?

_____

_____

_____

Giving a sincere compliment is a wonderful way to reach out to others. I'm not talking about buttering up someone, but noticing and recognizing the effort and work of others. If you make other people look good, you make yourself look good, too.

Receive compliments with similar sincerity and grace. Never disregard a compliment or suggest a person's opinion is wrong. "Pat, you look great in that suit." If Pat replies, "Oh, this old thing? Are you kidding? I look awful today," how is the person giving the compliment going to feel? Probably put down and a little foolish. Why argue with someone's point of view, especially if it's a positive view of you?

Included in the art of making small talk and conversing with others in social situations is diplomacy. Frederick Sawyer once said a diplomat is "…a man who thinks twice and says nothing." That's a good reminder if you're wondering what's okay to say. Noncommittal, general conversation is always a safe approach when you're unfamiliar with those around you and uncertain of relationships.

Here is a list of safe topics and a list of topics it is best to avoid:

Safe Topics

- Personal interests

- Travel

- Children

- Movies

- Current events

- Hobbies

- Weather

- Sports

- Work or business

- Books

- Restaurants

- Family

- Pets

Topics to Avoid

- Off-color or racial, ethnic or sexual jokes

- Personal finances/income

- Divorce/affair

- Weight

- Age

- Mental and physical health

- Romance

- Religion

- Politics

Dining Etiquette—Food for Thought

We're often more at ease in situations if we know in advance how
to handle them. Here are some ways to handle various situations.

- If you need to remove something from your mouth while dining with others, remove it the way it went in—and do it discreetly

- If you're ready to order, close the menu and signal the waiter.

- If you plan on sharing an entree, ask the server to have it prepared and split in the kitchen and served on two plates.

- If you are unsure about how to pronounce something on the menu, ask the server to help you or point it out on the menu.

- If you are hosting the function, be sure to tell people what attire is appropriate. If you are a guest, be sure to ask.

- If you aren't sure which utensil to use, work from the outside in and watch what others do.

- If you drop a piece of silverware on the floor, leave it there and tell your server.

- If you need to leave the table during a meal, excuse yourself and leave; there's no need to announce where you're going.

- If you want to make sure you get the check, make arrangements in advance.

- If you're not sure in what price range you should order, check to see what others are considering or what the host recommends.

- If someone has food on his or her face, motion to that person to indicate that he or she should wipe his/her face or kindly tell him or her.

- If you think your bill is wrong, go over to your server and question it. Do not make a scene about the bill in front of your guest.

- If you find something on your plate (a bug, hair, etc.), discreetly tell your server.

- If you have something stuck in your teeth, don't attempt to remove it at the table; excuse yourself and take care of it in the rest room.

- Unless you are expecting a very important call, do not bring your pager, cellular telephone, etc. to a restaurant. If it were to ring in the middle of a conversation, it would be disturbing and awkward for the person/s with you.

- If something is wrong with your meal, discreetly notify your server without causing a scene and making others uncomfortable.

- Never belch.

- If you need to bring out papers, wait until the dishes have been cleared and ask permission from the person you're with.

- If you feel a sneeze coming on, turn away from the table and sneeze into a napkin or tissue. Don't blow your nose at the table; it's very unappetizing for those around you.

Ordering and Paying the Tab

Once you're seated with your party, close your menu to show you're ready to order. The host orders last, the guest first. If you're the host, let your guest know what you're considering ordering or make recommendations. This isn't the time to order soup only or the diet plate, as your guest will feel compelled to follow your lead and order lightly. If you're the guest, order something in a medium price range.

If you're picking up the tab, let your server know beforehand that you want to pay. You can also arrive early, give the server your credit card in advance. Tell him or her to add a 15 or 20% gratuity and sign the receipt in advance so the server never has to present a bill. It's appropriate to check the bill for accuracy, but do it briefly and without drawing attention to it. Mentally calculate approximately what the bill will be as each person orders so you can spot a large discrepancy in the bill without hauling out your calculator. If you do suspect an error, take the bill to your server (away from the table) to review it.

Business can begin immediately after ordering, when the menus are put away. But don't miss the special opportunity that sharing a meal gives you to build rapport with business clients and colleagues. Start out with some small talk and, depending on the amount of time you have, gradually build to the business part of the meal. If the main purpose of the meal is social, let the work wait until after you eat.

At the Table: Tableware, Napkin, Passing, Eating

A place setting can be informal (a standard fork, knife and spoon) to formal (including eight or nine pieces of silverware). The best rule is to work from the outside in, because generally the silverware is placed according to the courses, or what is going to be served first, second, third, etc. If in doubt about which piece of silver to use, watch what others are doing and do the same.

Always put your napkin on your lap, with the crease toward you, as soon as you're seated. This way you won't forget to do it when the food is served. Use your napkin to blot or dab your face, not wipe. As mentioned earlier, if you leave your place during the meal, place your napkin on your chair. It isn't necessary to explain where you're going. A simple "Excuse me" is fine.

You'll always find the bread/butter or salad plate on your left and beverages on your right. Make sure to remember this so you don't eat or drink someone else's food or beverage! When asked to pass the salt, pass both the salt and pepper together.

You might be served "finger foods"—meant to be eaten with the fingers. French fries, hot dogs and sandwiches should be eaten this way. However, if French fries are served with other fork foods, use a fork to eat them. Break off, butter and eat small portions of bread or rolls rather than butter the whole roll and bringing it to your mouth to eat.

If you need to remove something from your mouth, remove it the way it went in. If you put the food in with a fork, remove it with a fork; if you put it in with your fingers, remove it with your fingers. Try to remove food without drawing attention to your action.

Keep your elbows off the table, hold your utensils properly (don't grab them, hold them like a shovel or clutch them) and never shovel food into your mouth. When you've finished eating, gently resting your elbows on the table to lean toward the conversation is fine and, in fact, conveys interest.

Although it might be the safest place, a briefcase doesn't belong on the table. Put it on your lap or between your feet for safekeeping. Be careful about putting it on the floor next to you because it may not be out of the way.

Potentially embarrassing problems while dining can be averted by reacting quickly and discreetly. For example, if someone you're dining with has food on his or her face or teeth, subtly motion to the person to wipe it away, or kindly tell him or her. Move on in conversation. If you find something unpleasant on your plate such as a hair or a bug, discreetly tell your waiter without interrupting the flow of conversation at the table.

If a quick check of your bill indicates it's been totaled up incorrectly, question it away from the table if at all possible. Take it over to your server or stand up when the server approaches you and turn away so your guests can continue talking. If service is slow or poor, the wrong item is served or the food is not prepared as ordered, again be assertive but discreet. It will not enhance your image to make a scene in a restaurant or embarrass a server in front of your guests, no matter how much it might be deserved.

To Drink or Not To Drink

A single glass of wine or one drink might be acceptable, but watch what others are doing. If no one else is drinking, don't. In fact, it is best in all business situations to avoid drinking altogether. If you need to drive yourself home, don't drink. If you need a good reason not to drink, the fact that you will be driving is a great one and admirable! Not only could doing so cost you your reputation, but your life. Too often, even a small amount of alcohol can loosen your tongue. Alcohol use makes it easier to say, do, or even imply something that casts a bad light on you. Why risk it? Even if others drink, moderately or heavily, watch your alcohol intake. *Self control and restraint are characteristics of success*—in office politics, business negotiations or personal conduct.

Be aware that how you handle drinking conveys impressions that you sometimes can't control. The safest bet is not to drink, or, if others are ordering, to order a single drink, sip it slowly, and stop at one.

Points to Remember

1. Develop state-of-the-art conversation skills, including listening and talking ability.

2. Know, practice and keep yourself updated on dining and other social etiquette matters including ordering, tipping and picking up the tab.

3. Limit your intake of alcohol or simply forego alcohol altogether.

How You Can Gain
the Professional Edge

How to Gain the Professional Edge covers many important issues, starting with who you are and where you want to go. While the details of personal appearance are important to gaining that edge, being successful encompasses far more.

By reading this book, you've been given the tools to create and convey a professional IMAGE in every one of five key areas:

Impression

Movement

Attitude

Grooming

Etiquette

You have the power to achieve your own professional edge. Now it's up to *you* to make these principles work. If you are willing to be open to others, open to their feedback, and open to change,

I guarantee you'll have every opportunity to excel in today's challenging business environment—and enjoy the process! Your attitude and openness will determine the way others respond to you. In order to bring out the best in others, you first need to bring out the best in *yourself.*

Recently, I was asked to present the closing session of an all-day conference. My task was to tie together the day's activities and motivate those in attendance to put the information they had gathered that day to use in their own lives. I knew I would be dealing with a group of tired people at the end of a long day, so I decided to try something new. I created an evaluation for them to fill out, not just on me, the speaker, but on *themselves* as well.

"How did *you* come across today?" I asked. "Open-minded? Attentive? Friendly?" Some of the attendees began to sit up and shift in their chairs.

"Did you give your undivided attention to the speakers? Were you participating 100 percent?"

I pointed out how easy it is to evaluate others, to be full of opinions and advice for them, and even to judge them rather harshly. But how honest are most of us about evaluating *ourselves?* Here are some things to think about.

- We all have bad days. But the people with whom we resonate are those who are positive, upbeat, and make us feel good. You can be one of those people whom others like to have around, even on a bad day. You might have to act like you feel terrific until you really do feel terrific. It works—try it! Sometimes you need to push yourself and "act" upbeat even if you don't feel it, but in no time at all, you *will* feel it.

- What impact do you want to make? What do you want people to think of when your name comes up? *The people who leave a lasting impression on us are often those who exceed our expectations.*

I have run into people long after they participated in my program and I am always interested to hear the things they tell me.

- "I changed my hairstyle"

- "I always remember to pass the salt and pepper together"

- "I only wear dark colors now"

- "I always wear a jacket"

- "I've remembered to shake with two pumps"

- "I try to be more optimistic and positive."

What interests me most is how every person picks up something different from the same workshop. They personalize it. And though initially my reaction has sometimes been, "Is that all you remember?" I am thrilled to hear there are one or two things people pick up because I know I have reached them in some way. I have realized that walking away with just one or two ideas is a huge step in the self-improvement process. People can't change who they are overnight. It often happens in small steps.

- Gaining the professional edge is not a one-shot, overnight thing. It's a long-term commitment to looking at yourself honestly and objectively, being open to constructive comments, and creating and refining your professional image every day. Will you make that commitment?

- Gaining the professional edge is within your grasp— and your future. With the confidence and strategies you have developed by reading this book, you can remake yourself to become that person with the extra professional edge. It only takes twenty-one days to make or break a habit. Why not start making changes today?

Think about how much more effective our workplaces would be and the better service we would receive if everyone with whom we come into contact used the principles in this book. As you continue to put the principles of this book into practice, measure your progress every day.

I'd like to know what your reaction is to the book and how it has affected you. I always enjoy hearing the ways people are able to use some of my ideas or about a point that made a difference. If you have a success story or are struggling with something, please let me hear from you. Although I cannot promise to respond to each letter personally, I may be able to use my column to address a problem you're having.

Remember:

- You can create and project the professional image you want to project

- You can manage the message you send

- **You can Gain the Professional Edge!**

Image Check List

Impression:
- ✓ Firm handshake—two pumps
- ✓ Eye contact—long enough to remember eye color
- ✓ Smile

Movement:
- ✓ Walk with a confident stride
- ✓ Maintain upright posture
- ✓ Hold head high
- ✓ Use controlled, broad gestures
- ✓ Open hands, body

Attitude:
- ✓ Positive
- ✓ Pleasant
- ✓ Enthusiastic

Grooming:
- ✓ Clean/spot and stain-free
- ✓ Well pressed
- ✓ Stockings neutral or tinted to match hem
- ✓ Proper fit
- ✓ Darker colors for authority
- ✓ Shoes darker than or same as hem color
- ✓ Skirt length neither too short (more than two to three inches above knee) nor too long (at or near the floor)
- ✓ Shoes/briefcase polished and in good condition
- ✓ Silhouette looks good from all angles in full length mirror
- ✓ Hands well groomed
- ✓ Breath fresh
- ✓ Updated, neat hair style
- ✓ Make-up subtle, well-blended

Etiquette:
- ✓ Avoid gossip
- ✓ Return calls within one business day
- ✓ Introduce most honored person first
- ✓ Avoid controversial topics
- ✓ Take an interest in others
- ✓ Focus on making others feel comfortable
- ✓ Limit alcohol

About the Author

Susan Morem is founder and president of Premier Presentation, Inc., a Minneapolis-based training and consulting firm. She has addressed audiences all over the United States on a wide variety of topics related to personal and professional development. Her client list includes many Fortune 500 companies, including AAA, Aetna, Citibank, Coca-Cola, Control Data, Honeywell, Inc. IBM, 3M, and Target Stores.

Susan has been a frequent guest on many radio and television programs. She has been featured in numerous publications, including *The Wall Street Journal, USA Today,* the Minneapolis-St. Paul *Star Tribune,* the *Pioneer Press,* the *Dallas Morning News,* the *Asbury Park Press, Glamour* magazine, *Personnel News,* and *Training Magazine.* She is the author of the popular *Business Casual Handbook* and two internationally distributed videos, *The Power of Professionalism* and *Business Casual.* Susan also writes a weekly syndicated workplace/business advice column that is featured in newspapers across the country.

She presents her programs at company meetings, half-day workshops and full-day seminars.

In addition to her work within companies, Susan is often a keynote speaker at association meetings, conventions and trade shows.

Susan is married and the mother of three daughters. In her leisure time she enjoys spending time with her family and their dog, Alex.

To bring Susan Morem to your company, conference, convention or association gathering, contact:

Premier Presentation, Inc.
10700 Highway 55, Suite 220
Plymouth, Minnesota 55441
Phone: (612) 540-0670
E-mail: mzbizniz@aol.com.

Order Form

Please send me _____ copy (copies) of *How to Gain the Professional Edge* by Susan Morem, at a cost of $17.95 each (includes a $3.00 shipping and handling cost.) (In Minnesota, add sales tax for a total of $18.93 per book.)

☐ Check enclosed for _____

☐ Bill my credit card (Visa or Mastercard)

      Card Number _____

      Expiration Date _____

      Signature _____ Date _____

Name _____

Company _____

Address _____

City _____ State _____ Zip _____

☐ Yes, I would like the book(s) autographed to:

_____

_____

_____

Mail or fax to:

      Premier Presentation, Inc.

      10700 Highway 55, Suite 220

      Plymouth, Minnesota 55441

      Phone: (612) 540-0670

      Fax: (612) 557-5170